The Modern Rockhounding and Prospecting Handbook

GARRET ROMAINE

FALCONGUIDES

GUILFORD, CONNECTICUT
HELENA, MONTANA

AN IMPRINT OF ROWMAN & LITTLEFIELD

FalconGuides is an imprint of Rowman & Littlefield.
Falcon, FalconGuides, and Outfit Your Mind are registered trademarks of Rowman & Littlefield.

Photos by Garret Romaine unless otherwise noted
Distributed by NATIONAL BOOK NETWORK

Library of Congress Cataloging-in-Publication Data is available on file.

ISBN 978-0-7627-8470-7

Printed in the United States of America

To my Dad, Garret L. Romaine,
who was always ready to jump in the rig and head for the hills.

CONTENTS

PREFACE

The purpose of this guide is to set you on a path for success in collecting geological specimens in the field. Whether you want to find rocks, minerals, fossils, precious metals, or meteorites, this book is for you. Beginners of all types and levels of expertise will benefit from the information here about what to look for, how to research an area, and what to do with your treasures.

Intermediate, experienced rockhounds and prospectors will benefit from this guide as well. The sections on modern research and tools should be of interest to anyone who has been out a few times and wants to improve his or her chances. I've been tracking the Internet for almost twenty years, starting a regular column for Gold Prospectors Association of America in 1997 titled "Mining the Internet." I shared with readers interesting sites they needed to check out to improve their tactics and techniques and help make them better rockhounds. Many of those columns and articles inspired this book.

I've included several sidebars where experts talk about putting it all together. If you truly love being outdoors, stalking collectibles, and talking about rocks, you should consider taking your hobby to the next level. These experts demonstrate various career directions you could investigate to see whether you can make a living out of what you love.

This book is organized into five chapters:

1. **What to Look For**—You'll get a basic overview of the geological forces of interest to us hobbyists, such as how plate tectonics affect economic ore deposits and how a smattering of geological principles can come in handy. In addition you'll find a list of the most common rocks, minerals, crystals, fossils, and metals that should spur your expeditions.

2. **Where to Find It**—Once you have an idea of what you want to bring home, you need to be able to put together a basic plan on where to track it down. Some areas, such as the Obsidian Needles Mine in northern California, have so much plentiful material that it is literally laying on the ground as soon as you step out of your vehicle. But other areas require some serious mapping, researching, and studying. You may need to do some Internet research, including social networking sites, in order to connect with others who have been to the spot you want to search.

3. **How to Get It Home**—Now that you have a plan, you need to mount your expedition. Just heading for the beach to look for agates is easy enough, but you might be interested in some tools that can save your back a lot of wear and tear. If you are more ambitious and want to explore an old mining district with plenty of tailings, you may need all-terrain vehicles (ATVs) and a trailer. If you don't like sleeping in a tent, you might want an RV. This section includes information on electronic prospecting with ultraviolet lights, metal detectors, and magnets, as well as such tools as sluices, panning wheels, and other devices.

4. **Working in the Field**—Once you reach the locale or district that you've been planning to visit, your work begins. This section contains information about the wide variety of tools and devices available, covers some of the legal restrictions in place, and takes you through simple walks at the beach to working on ledges, veins, and vugs. You'll find tips and pointers for rockhounding, gold prospecting, fossil hunting, and metal detecting.

5. **What to Do with It**—Once you start bringing home better and better trophies, you will want to learn how to show them off. Small quartz crystals make excellent jewelry, as do other showy gems. You can knap obsidian into arrowheads, spear points, and jewelry; you can carve soapstone into fetishes, amulets, and statues. This chapter also contains basic information about traditional lapidary, faceting, wire-wrapping, fashioning cabochons, and more.

ACKNOWLEDGMENTS

A special thanks to all who provided input for this handbook, but especially to Val Bailey, Frank Higgins, Kevan Reedy, Martin Schippers, Terry Snider, and Dirk Williams, who each proved once again to be practical and helpful in the field and encouraging in their comments—all layered with a healthy skepticism for someone who overplans and overpacks.

INTRODUCTION

There's no easy definition of a rockhound. Generally, a rockhound will pick up just about any geological treasure and bring it home. They can be interested in rocks, gems, gold, fossils, and meteorites—all at the same time.

So then, what is a prospector? According to www.wikianswers.com, "A prospector is someone who explores for minerals or other valuable resources for profit or sometimes just as a hobby. Prospecting involves physical labor looking for any trace of the sought after mineral."

We'll come back to the "physical labor" part in a little bit. Meanwhile, here's another way to figure out where you fit:

A **casual observer** is someone who enjoys camping and road trips, but rarely picks up anything to bring home.

A **pebble pup** is a camper who usually comes home with at least one pretty rock in his or her pocket.

A **rockhound** brings a bucket and other tools and comes home with much more material than the pebble pup.

A **prospector** finds so much material that it might be time to consider filing a claim.

A **field geologist** can select from several claims and figure out which one to put into production.

A **mining engineer** will devise the production plan for that mine.

Casual Observer	Pebble Pup	Rockhound	Prospector	Field Geologist	Mining Engineer

If you've ever looked at the cliffs and tried to figure them out, or if you've ever smashed a rock with a hammer and had an idea of what you were looking for, you're no longer a pebble pup. If you've ever purposefully looked for something valuable and started to dig a big hole, you're on your way to becoming a modern rockhound or prospector. Finally, if you've ever thought about staking a claim or starting a mine, you could have a real future.

Most of us are somewhere between Pebble Pup and Field Geologist, no matter what we're after. Rockhounds often spend more time walking than digging, searching beaches and gravel bars or walking the desert. Advanced rockhounds bang on tailings or dig out veins and vugs. Gold panners spend most of their time in the water, but advanced prospectors search for ledges and veins still encased in rock. Fossil diggers rarely collect much from the surface, save for concretions, and need to understand a lot more geology to track down prime strata for their prizes. Meteorite hunters may collect on the surface, walking great distances, or dig for targets found with their metal detector. Notice how all of this requires physical labor? That's a trend that will continue.

We would all like to get out more, no matter what our level. Collecting geological specimens is fun, and it's a great excuse to plan a road trip. Mounting a successful expedition requires planning, patience, adaptability, and a lot of free time. But it's a noble cause. Your search is for the missing link, the key bit of evidence, the true discovery. You could find a new species of dinosaur and name it for your mom. You could chance upon a never-before-seen meteorite and add to the annals of science. You could discover a new mineral or spark a modern-day gold rush. With the current interest in modern exploration and prospecting, new discoveries are more possible today than at any time since the West was opened up. Once you get good at it, you could take your skills all over the world, looking for whatever you feel passionate about.

When possible, considerate collectors leave something for the next person. But there's a fine line between leaving something for the next person and letting it go to waste:

1. Agates continually get pulverized by rushing water and the tumbling tide and are eventually reduced to tiny grains of sand.

2. Water and time reduce gold nuggets to flakes, and flakes become particles, until eventually gold particles are so small they dissolve into seawater.

3. Fossil collecting is mostly search and rescue; erosion will eventually obliterate even a whale skull in a concretion.

4. Because of their high iron content, meteorites are very susceptible to oxidation. Unless they land in the dry desert, most meteorites

that reach the Earth's surface will rust away in just a few thousand years.

Thanks to the Internet, you don't have to be a generalist and try to get one of everything. You can specialize, zeroing in on the specimens that interest you most. You can easily find like-minded people who share your enthusiasm and might even join you on your expeditions. This book will help you do just that.

As much fun as it is to get out and explore the old mining districts and ghost towns of yesteryear, a growing collection will be proof that you know what you are doing. Beginner's luck should eventually give way to expertise, and then you can share your expertise with others and help them be successful too.

If uncovering Mother Nature's secrets was easy, there wouldn't be many mysteries left to solve. But scientists still have lots of questions, and sometimes it feels as though we're trying to solve a puzzle without having all the pieces. We feel constantly thwarted by the mythical creature North American Indians named Coyote the Trickster, who set clever traps and delighted in tormenting human beings. A lot of the time, he wins—but not always.

With help from the websites, mailing lists, blogs, and social media now available, your chances of gathering interesting specimens is greater than ever. You have much greater access now to expert advice, veteran collectors, and spot-on descriptions to aid you while you research and while you work in the field. So happy hunting out there, and good luck!

CHAPTER 1
WHAT TO LOOK FOR

The quality, beauty, and value of earthly treasures available to even casual collectors is a source of constant amazement. Thanks to the advantage of living on a young planet with active geological forces, we are surrounded by deposits of rocks, minerals, fossils, and metals that inspire artists, jewelers, craftspeople, miners, and collectors all over the world. We are truly blessed—the geological wonders awaiting us are awe-inspiring in their breadth and scope. Whether you are an infrequent agate picker at the beach, a weekend gold panner up in the mountains, a budding fossil digger curious about early life forms, or a would-be meteorite hunter hoping to find rocks from space, this book will help improve your odds of success.

The more you know about geology and other earth sciences, the better your chances of success in the field. Knowing some key fundamentals will improve your odds as you venture out. If you remember anything from your science courses as a kid, you know that geology isn't just a single discipline; it borrows heavily from biology, chemistry, physics, and math. You have to be a bit of a generalist to excel at geology, which is part of its charm.

Consider the great German geographer, geologist, naturalist, and scientist Friedrich Wilhelm Heinrich Alexander von Humboldt (1769–1859). Von Humboldt left an outsize imprint on whatever he touched; he didn't just note how certain plants grew at certain zones, he practically invented the field of biogeography. His immense work *Kosmos* (1845) set out to unify the various squabbling and competing branches of science. He anticipated continental drift by about 150 years, and his epic five-year voyage to the Americas culminated in a sleepover at the White House as a guest of President Jefferson. His trips led to advances in physical geography, meteorology, volcanism, magnetism, and more.

Alexander von Humboldt was a superb field worker and one of the great general scientists in history.

Today von Humboldt's name graces a bay in Northern California, the main current off the west coast of South America, a glacier in Greenland, a sink in Nevada, and a mountain in Venezuela. He also named a tree, skunk, squid, penguin, and orchid, among many other things. One of the greatest general scientists ever, he started at an early age when he wrote a treatise on the mineralogy of various basalts along the Rhine River. There was so much to learn at that time that he didn't get to concentrate on geology, but *you* have that luxury.

BASIC GEOLOGY

We know that Earth's core is a nickel-iron metal; the next zone, the mantle, is believed to be a plastic, melted mixture. As collectors, we are mostly interested in the Earth's crust, the thin veneer of rock exposed to the atmosphere and riding on the mantle. Geologists estimate that up to 80 percent of the rocks at the planet's surface are sedimentary. But the farther you go down, the quicker you leave the sedimentary rocks behind, as heat and pressure turn mudstones into argillite and turn basalt into greenstone. We think that metamorphic rocks make up 85 percent of the crust, with sedimentary rocks only 8 percent of the total volume. That leaves 7 percent for igneous rocks.

According to a 1980 paper by J. W. Morgan and E. Anders titled "Chemical Composition of Earth, Venus, and Mercury," Earth's composition is dominated by iron, as shown in Table 1.

Table 1. Chemical Composition of the Earth

Element	Percentage
Iron	32.1%
Oxygen	30.1
Silicon	15.1
Magnesium	13.9
Sulfur	2.9
Nickel	1.8
Calcium	1.5
Aluminum	1.4
All others	1.2

Later in the same article, the work of geochemist F. W. Clark points to the Earth's crust being 60 percent silica for continental crust and 49 percent silica for oceanic crust. That's good news for mineral hunters who like quartz crystals.

To become competent in the field, you need to be able to recognize the common rocks you are walking on and looking at and know the different opportunities for collecting that each type of rock represents. So let's look again at the three major rock groups and consider their importance to collectors.

Sedimentary

Sedimentary rocks are the most favored by fossil diggers, as shales, mudstones, siltstones, and sandstones all offer opportunities for fossil collecting. Geologists who study ancient life are called paleontologists, and they frequently use advanced geological techniques to interpret field relationships. Even amateur fossils diggers can learn geologic mapping to determine the age of the rocks they wish to hunt, narrowing their search.

Limestones are noted for fossils, but rockhounds know that these calcium carbonates frequently host attractive calcite and gypsum crystals. Flint nodules are common in some chalk deposits, and chert layers can form in sandstones. Gold prospectors exploit sands and gravels in their search for gold, and some miners look for older, cemented gravels that reveal ancient river systems. Meteorite hunters tend to favor dry lakebeds in the desert for the color contrast as well as the low humidity.

Basically, sedimentary rocks offer something for everyone.

Igneous

Lava fields contain unusual collecting opportunities. The ropy texture of some flows makes for a nice display rock, and volcanic bombs are worth bringing home. Basalt columns make beautiful displays and fountains when perfectly formed. In between layers of rhyolite, andesite, or basalt, geologists often identify beds of tuff and ash that contain petrified wood and leaf fossils. Obsidian is probably the most highly prized igneous rock, especially when it comes in various sheens and colors. Agates occasionally form in the bubbles at the top of some basalt flows, and sunstones form in certain lavas.

Topaz crystals form in vugs and cavities in igneous rocks. Zeolites are common in cracks and vugs in igneous rocks. Quartz crystals are often present in veins, especially as drusy coatings. Pegmatites, intrusive structures that cool slowly, are probably the most sought-after

All of the Above, Please

W. Dan Hausel has had many professional titles, including Senior Economic Geologist, Vice President of Exploration, and now Independent Consulting Geologist. Famed in Wyoming for his discovery of numerous economic deposits, he is also a prolific author.

I'm what you call a polymath. This affliction drove my teachers crazy when I was young. I could never focus on one thing (still can't). Prior to college, many of my teachers figured I was a problem because I constantly daydreamed. Prior to our high school graduation, my parents were summoned to the school by my counselor. She told my parents it would be a waste of money to send me to college as I had no aptitude for higher education and they should instead think about steering me toward military enlistment. But college was one place to help stimulate my curiosities and dreams.

Luckily, I went to college and earned BS and MS degrees in geology while working initially as an astronomy lecturer at a major planetarium. I was able to convince the director of the planetarium that even though I was a self-trained astronomer and had no public speaking experience, I would be very good at this job. And I was. Later, I left this job to work on a project in the geology department researching lunar rocks that had been collected by Neil Armstrong and other astronauts. At the same time, I was playing lead guitar in a rock-and-roll band on weekends and was president of the university's karate club. That's what they call a polymath.

igneous rocks, as the large crystal structures in these intrusive dikes host beryl, emeralds, sapphires, and other gems. Layered granitic intrusions that cool slowly at depth and give minerals time to form can also create zones of rich metallic ores.

Metamorphic

Metamorphic rocks tend to have large crystals, due to slow, constant reheating at depth in the Earth's crust. Kyanite, staurolite, and garnet all indicate different levels of heat and pressure; all are collectible crystals. Quartz crystals are common in metamorphic rocks, as are calcite crystals. There is very little fossil collecting in metamorphic rocks, as heat and pressure tend to deform fossils. Gold prospecting is much more rewarding in older metamorphic rocks—especially when large granitic intrusions have melted through older terrains. The contact zones between older metamorphic rocks and younger intrusions often host quartz veins with economic ore deposits.

RESOURCES FOR BASIC GEOLOGY

Think of it this way: The Earth is spinning around the sun, revolving on a solid nickel-iron inner core, with a gooey liquid zone next, and then a crispy outer shell. Spinning on that metal ball gives us magnetism, our size gives us gravity, and the generated heat keeps the middle melted and moving. The heat transfers send plumes of hot, liquid rock bursting through to the surface as volcanoes or freezing in place as granitic intrusions. As long as the internal engine keeps pumping, things keep moving. Eventually planets get old and cold as their sun cools, and even galaxies collapse around some peculiar drain. But for now, we have the best of all possible worlds—young, active, and interesting.

There are several online resources available to help improve your insights into geology and help you become a better field collector. Your ability to teach yourself (or maybe just remind yourself) of the main principles of geology will help you out immensely.

Basic Geology Websites

The website **www.geology.com** is one of the best places to bookmark for return visits if you are just starting out trying to understand geologic concepts and terms. Or maybe you need a refresher? Still unclear on how pegmatites form? Try the teacher resources at http://geology.com/teacher for smart, well-built modules on topics you want to understand.

WikiBooks has a growing introduction to basic geology at http://en.wikibooks.org/wiki/Basic_Geology. It's a good starting point, but it needs more beef in several areas.

Wikipedia has a ton of information about all the key principles of geology at http://en.wikipedia.org/wiki/Outline_of_geology. They do an excellent job with citations and additional links, in case you want to dive deeper into some key points of economic geology or mineral formation.

The **US Geological Survey (USGS)** has excellent educational resources for all levels at http://education.usgs.gov/secondary.html#geology. These resources are built to serve teachers up to the university level, although they are most valuable to junior high and high school kids. The USGS is particularly helpful when it comes to mapping, map symbols, and learning about geographic information systems (GIS).

About.com is a rich jumping-off point for learning geology; start at http://geology.about.com and follow the links. Author Andrew Alden has a patient, thoughtful approach to explaining topics and keeps the site fresh with constant articles that update the flow of information. His "Wine and Rocks" article, for example, explained the relationship between the right soils, optimal drainage, and your favorite grape beverage.

Geology Rocks has a good overview of the principles of geology at www.geologyrocks.co.uk/tutorials/introduction_to_geology. It is written in an informative, helpful style, and you can go deeper into topics as you need to. The site gets technical quickly, but if you can keep up, you can learn a lot.

The **Geological Society of America** has an excellent website. Check out www.geosociety.org, and consider joining the organization.

Planetary Geology

If you already know the basics of geology, one more area to conquer is the fastest-growing field of rock and mineral studies: planetary geology. By placing robotic exploration vehicles on the surface of Mars, we are learning to solve geological riddles on a bigger scale. The concepts we solidify by landing on the surface of other planets and moons, capturing interplanetary stardust, and returning samples from comets is all geologically significant.

Your understanding of the planet Earth has to mesh with your knowledge of planetary geology in general. You need a sense for not only Earth's mechanics but also the basic way *all* planets appear to be put together. This field helps you understand the concept of a planetary core, how the crust covers up an active mantle, and how continents move around. It can make you feel smart, and make you feel small.

Here are a few sites to get you at least comfortable with the terms used by planetary geologists.

Jet Propulsion Laboratory is still running the older Mars Rover program, with the Spirit and Opportunity robots, and there is a lot of planetary geology information available at http://marsrovers.jpl.nasa.gov/home/index.html. However, most of the action is at the new site tracking the Curiosity rover: http://mars.jpl.nasa.gov/msl.

Wikipedia is always a great place to start: Search on common terms like "planetary geology" and "geology of the moon" to start loading uplinks. You'll find many updated articles pertaining to the geology of various planets and moons, and you'll start to get a feel for the basics. There are links to major institutions around the world that study space, planetary science, geophysics, asteroids, and more. You can start at their planetary geology page or jump right to planetary science at http://en.wikipedia.org/wiki/Planetary_science.

NASA (the National Aeronautics and Space Administration) has targeted teaching materials for various grade levels. Here's a link to their Planetary Geology module, a 223-page download: www.nasa.gov/audience/foreducators/topnav/materials/listbytype/Planetary.Geology.html.

Geology Apps

Whether you connect to the Internet via a smart phone, tablet, laptop, notebook, or other lightweight portable device, there is an information explosion under way, thanks to the availability of software applications, or "apps," that are for sale or free. Here are some places you can bookmark and keep coming back to in your quest for more knowledge of geology. Use their search features to find new apps that can help you understand what kind of geological specimens to look for.

Apple Store
www.apple.com/iphone

You'll come to a screen with a magnifying glass to enter search terms. Type in "geology" and search on the term—you'll see, for example, an app for the Minerals Database at www.mindat.org.

AppUp
www.appup.com/app-details/science3-rocks,-minerals-and-soils

The Intel AppUp Center has loads of resources, many for a modest fee, such as $0.99. The Science3 Rocks, Minerals, and Soils app looked interesting for junior high students.

Apps Zoom
www.appszoom.com/android_applications/minerals

Apps Zoom offers free and for-purchase apps. The company offers a solid list of fossil identification and fossil collecting apps, lists several mineral identification apps, and has the most common geology apps. There is also a gold prospecting app, but under "meteorites" there are mostly games involving shooting meteorites.

EasyLearn Earth Science
One app of note is EasyLearn Earth Science: Structure of Earth. More for kids to learn about the structure of Earth, it is written in plain terms and easy for all ages to follow. The facts are presented in a very simple manner with lots of pictures. You can learn the facts, practice what you learned, and then take the quiz and check your answers.

POPULAR COLLECTIBLES
Use this list as a starting point to figure out what you are most interested in collecting. It is by no means exhaustive. About 10,000 different minerals have been identified so far, but the following are some of the common rocks and minerals you will hear other collectors talk about the most.

Agate is a loosely defined term for a gem-quality chalcedony and is the most collectible quartz. It is translucent, meaning light passes through, and can appear as chunks of glass when at least partially tumbled in streams and beach gravels. Unlike pure, crystalline quartz, which forms in hexagonal crystals, agate features banding and impurities and shows no crystalline structure. Agate often forms at the top of lava flows, hardening inside bubbles in the basalt, or sometimes forms as seams between lava flows. Carnelian, a light to dark red-orange variety of

agate, is highly collectible. Some blue forms of agate, such as Ellensburg blue (from Washington State) and Holley blue (from Oregon), are probably more properly classified as chalcedony but are most commonly called agates.

Agate is easily fashioned into cabochons, belt buckles, bolo ties, rings, necklaces, and earrings. When slabbed into thin sections, agate makes beautiful tables, countertops, and other displays. Agates show up in many beach gravels along the coast of North America, around Lake Superior in Minnesota, along the Missouri River, in Montana, and in numerous other locales.

Amber is a general term for many different types of fossilized tree resin. The science and classification of amber varieties is extensive, but there are only two main amber-collecting locales in the world: the Baltic Sea in northern Europe and the Dominican Republic. However, amber can be found in many other locales worldwide, identified on the World of Amber site: http://academic.emporia.edu/abersusa/geograph.htm.

The movie *Jurassic Park* popularized the idea of extracting DNA from insects trapped within amber. Consequently, amber specimens with trapped insects command a premium.

Amber is rare in North America, but deposits or discoveries have been reported in Kansas, California, Washington, New Jersey, Arkansas, and Alaska.

Ammolite is a fossilized ammonite shell restricted in geography to the eastern Rocky Mountains. The chemistry is complicated, but essentially the aragonite shell of the ammonite displays iridescence throughout the sheets of shell material. Green, red, blue, and violet colors seem to shimmer.

Ammolite was designated as an official gemstone in 1981. It is commercially mined from Cretaceous deposits that made up the Western Inland Sea—primarily from the Bearpaw Formation. Most deposits are located in Alberta and Saskatchewan, but gem-quality deposits exist in Montana and as far south as central Utah.

Apatite crystals are not common and thus are highly collectible if gem quality. This phosphate forms tabular, prismatic hexagonal crystals, but again, they are rare. Most commonly apatite is massive or granular and is mined for phosphate-based fertilizer. Varieties are blue, green, and clear and display some chatoyance (cat's-eye reflection), making for good cabochons. All collectors should keep at least one good sample of apatite in their field identification kit, as it is the defining mineral for 5 on the Mohs scale of hardness. Human teeth contain apatite, which provides more hardness than calcite. Best collecting opportunities include pegmatites, such as those found in the Keystone District of South Dakota's Black Hills; many other states have apatite deposits.

Aquamarine is a highly collectible variety of blue beryl that is not common in the United States. It is marked by pale blue, transparent to translucent hexagonal columnar crystals, but it can be brittle and is a challenge to work with. Also be aware that the color can fade over time. Aquamarine is usually associated with pegmatites. Two US deposits stand out—near the Powder River Pass in Wyoming's Bighorn Mountains and at the top of 14,276-foot Mount Antero in Colorado.

Aventurine, actually another form of quartz, is commonly green. Other colors include blue, orange, and brown. What makes aventurine stand out is its tendency to shimmer or glisten, thanks to the presence of small, platy mica crystals. This effect is called aventurescence. Because it is relatively hard, 6.5 on the Mohs scale, aventurine can be polished and thus used in most jewelry applications. It also makes for interesting and decorative yard rock; www.mindat.org shows deposits in Nebraska, West Virginia, and Vermont, associated with metamorphic rocks as a source of mica.

Azurite is an easy copper ore to spot because it isn't green malachite, which is much more common. Azurite is a stunning blue in comparison.

The two are often but not always found together. Azurite is rarely carved or fashioned into designs, but it makes for stunning displays when found in velvety, botryoidal form. Many of the top specimens come from copper mines around Bisbee, Arizona.

Basalt is a common lava and not valued for much more than yard rock or for building modest walls in the garden. However, when basalt cools into large columns, it is valuable for large displays. You can drill a vertical hole through a large basalt column and turn it into a fountain. Smaller columnar basalt exposures, where the columns are less than a foot across, are easier to work with, and the hexagonal form is easy to slice into attractive coasters and tiles. Columnar basalt and colonnades are fairly common in basalt flows across North America.

Beryl is an aluminum silicate with beryllium in the crystal lattice. To find it, look for pegmatites, which are dikes and intrusions with very large crystals, either in vugs or in the veins themselves. Aquamarine, emerald, goshenite, and morganite are all forms of beryl. The hexagonal crystals of plain beryl are common in some pegmatites, but true gem-quality specimens are rare. California, South Dakota, Idaho, Colorado, North Carolina, and the New England states have yielded beryl-bearing pegmatites.

Emeralds are a green form of beryl, usually associated with certain pegmatites. Gem-quality emerald is rare; Columbia is the world leader in emerald production, although Zambia has recently produced more and more high-quality emeralds. North Carolina is the acknowledged leader in gem-quality North American emerald production, and there are several fee-dig operations around the state's Alexander County.

Calcite, or calcium carbonate, is quite common, and only a few forms are prized by collectors. Sharp, double-terminated crystals are rare but possible. Calcite usually forms as small encrustations like quartz, but they are not hexagonal, favoring dogtooth or nail spar habits; some of

these plates are worth collecting as display pieces. Calcite is usually slightly yellow, so clear, pure calcite rhombs are noteworthy. In addition, clear rhombs show an interesting double refraction; if you place an image under a good calcite specimen, you'll see two copies of the image. Prospectors soon learn to recognize that the two important angles for calcite crystal faces are 74 and 55 degrees. Calcite is the defining mineral for 3 on the Mohs scale and thus should be a part of every collector's field identification kit. It is a ubiquitous mineral, present in sandstones, many igneous rocks, and some metamorphic rocks. Pure, clear calcite is known as Iceland spar and comes from deposits in Iceland, China, Mexico, and New Mexico.

Chalcedony is the main classification category of cryptocrystalline quartz, which has such a loosely identifiable rock structure of minute crystals that it may as well have no crystal structure. Some of the common, collectible forms of chalcedony include agate, aventurine, carnelian, chrysoprase, heliotrope, moss agate, and onyx. All forms are transparent to translucent and quite hard, 6 to 7 on the Mohs scale, and show no cleavage; they have a common conchoidal fracture and a waxy luster that can range to vitreous, dull, greasy, or silky. Quartz is one of the most common minerals on the surface of the Earth, and the presence of chalcedony almost everywhere in one form or another is a big reason. Here's a good link from the USGS: http://minerals.usgs.gov/minerals/pubs/commodity/gemstones/sp14-95/chalcedony.html.

Fossil **concretions** are round masses of lime-rich material that typically form around organic debris in rocking tidal zones. Sticky clay builds up in a round shape due to rolling around in water. The majority of these round concretions are plain mud balls, having formed around something tiny. But some concretions

form around ammonites, shark teeth, crab skeletons, seal vertebrae, and whale skulls. Fossils found inside concretions are usually protected from erosion and well preserved. Eastern Wyoming is noted for large concretions bearing big ammonites; many Cenozoic sedimentary rocks, especially in coastal zones, play host to these rocks. There are numerous other locales in sedimentary deposits across North America, especially along the continent's west coast.

Copper is rarely found in elemental "nuggets"; even coppery stringers are rare, as they oxidize quickly. Large hunks of pure native copper make for attractive display pieces but are easy to simulate, so beware. Pure, native copper nuggets still show up on Michigan's Keweenaw Peninsula. Fee-digs, museums, parks, guided trips, camping—there are Internet links galore for copper collecting in the Upper Peninsula of Michigan: www.exploring thenorth.com/rocks/collect.html.

Diamonds are rare but not completely out of the question. Believe it or not, there are a few opportunities to rockhound and prospect for diamonds in North America. Diamonds are closely associated with kimberlite, a dark gray to blue igneous rock known to be found in Kimberley, South Africa. Kimberlite pipes apparently extrude at the Earth's surface from far below and form as circular dikes. Being susceptible to erosion, these pipes often appear at the surface as round ponds or small lakes, and diamond miners have learned to track down these pipes by searching for diamondiferous kimberlite and screening for the exotic garnets associated with these rocks. Wyoming offers several areas where kimberlite pipes have intruded into old Archean craton rock. Here's a link for prospecting in Wyoming: www .wsgs.uwyo.edu/research/minerals/Diamonds.aspx. Arkansas's famous Crater of Diamonds State Park has a fee-dig operation open to the public: www.craterofdiamondsstatepark.com.

Epidote is a light yellow to dark green mineral that makes nice display pieces when arranged as a coating of tiny crystals on igneous rocks. There are numerous varieties of epidote, as it is a common rock-forming silicate mineral with common elements such as calcium, aluminum, and iron. You can find epidote in metamorphic rocks such as schists and marbles, in igneous rocks, and rarely by itself as transparent, dark green crystals. Prince of Wales Island in British Columbia is a well-known source of "jackstraw" epidote, in which crystals fan out in a spray of dark green needles.

Flint is uncommon in North America; it is more common in Europe, where immense deposits of exquisite quality have yielded flint tools dating to Neolithic times. Knapping is the primary use for flint, now that flintlock rifles have fallen out of fashion. Think of flint as a variety of chert that originates in chalk or marly limestones, usually as nodules. Flint seems to form as an organic silica gel in limestone crevices. Look in known limestone areas in most of the eastern United States.

Fluorite is the defining mineral for a hardness of 4 on the Mohs scale, so every collector should have a nice crystal for testing between feldspar and calcite. Fluorite most commonly forms in the cubic mineral habit, forming attractive crystals. It is used in smelting iron, helping molten slag to flow more freely, but collectors know it for the phenomenon of fluorescence, where minerals glow in different colors under short- and long-wave black light. Many US states have fluorite deposits; it is the state mineral for Illinois, which at one time led the nation in fluorite production. Two other noted locales are Newfoundland's Burin Peninsula and the Rock Candy Mine near Grand Forks, British Columbia, which is a fee-dig operation (www.rockcandymine.com).

Fossil hunters face a lot of hurdles. For example, it sounds like fun to go out and dig for dinosaur bones, but there are actually severe legal restrictions on collecting the remains of ancient reptiles on public land. Fossil vertebrates—animals with a skeletal backbone—are completely off-limits for amateurs working on public land. So unless you can hook up with an organized dig operated by professionals with all the right permits, that leaves fossil leaves, shells, and some teeth as "safe" for legal collecting on public lands. There are numerous world-famous fee-dig fossil fish quarries at Fossil Butte, near Kemmerer, Wyoming. A

prime one is the Ulrich Fossil Gallery (www.ulrichsfossilgallery.com). Florida's Peace River is famed for large shark teeth; Utah's Delta area has fee-dig trilobite quarries.

Garnets are common, but they are typically difficult to find intact. There are at least twenty varieties, of all different colors, and the crystal habit is usually a rhombic dodecahedron. If you know Greek, that means it can have up to twelve crystal faces, although some forms are simply cubic, or four-sided. Garnet varieties include gemmy almandine (deep reddish), spessartine (more orange to red), pyrope (deep red to black), grossular (green to brown, yellow, or red), and more. Because garnet fractures rather than cleaves, it makes for a good abrasive—every time it breaks down it creates another sharp edge. Red garnets were often mistaken for rubies by early prospectors, and the number of geographic features that were misnamed as Ruby Creek, Ruby Ridge, and Ruby Mountain is legion. Sometimes almandine garnets display a "star" of aligned rutile when polished correctly, as in those found at the USDA Forest Service fee-dig area at Emerald Creek, Idaho. Here's a link to the Idaho Panhandle National Forests, which run the operation: www .fs.usda.gov/recarea/ipnf/recarea/?recid=6927.

Geodes are round stones with crystal-lined cavities inside. The interior crystals are usually quartz and sometimes amethyst; calcite is

another common geode crystal. Crystal-lined geodes are a prize in many areas, but the most sought after are from Keokuk, Iowa. They even have their own web page at www.keokukiowa tourism.org/geode.htm. According to the site, the greatest abundance and variety of prized geodes are found in the Mississippian-age lower Keokuk Formation in a general zone around the intersection of the Mississippi and Des Moines Rivers. There is even a Geode State Park. The most common size of Keokuk geodes is about 3 to 4 inches across, but some reach 2 feet across and larger.

California, Arizona, Washington, Utah, and Nevada also have geode collecting locales. The California desert is a noted geode area. Riverside and Imperial Counties boast the famed Hauser geode beds at Wiley Well and the North Black Hills and Cinnamon geode beds.

Gold is found in two forms: lode and placer. Lode ore deposits refer to gold that is bound up in a quartz vein or some other kind of host rock. It's hard to get out but can make you rich. Placer gold is a piece of native metal, from nugget to flake to tiny pinprick, found in certain gravels and sands. Most beginning prospectors start out washing gravels for showings of native gold, either in a big shaker table, trommel, sluice box, dredge, or gold pan. All rockhounds and prospectors should have a gold pan, as it helps identify black sands, garnets, and gold. There are numerous different contraptions available for seriously working a placer gold deposit, but they all use gravity to trap gold at the bottom of a riffle, sluice, or carpeting while washing away lighter material. Lode gold, usually found in quartz or calcite veins, can be much richer, but it requires more hard work, and more capital, to recover.

One of the interesting things about placer gold is that you often create concentrates of heavy black sands first and then recover gold from there. You will always find black sands with placer gold, because all gravel deposits have some traces of magnetite, ilmenite, stardust, fishing weights, bullet fragments, and other debris. But you don't always find gold with those black sands, so you want to follow the first rule of gold prospecting: Gold is not where you find it; it's where it's already been found. The old prospectors pretty much dialed in all the biggest gold deposits across North America. But the second law of gold prospecting is just as important: They didn't get it all. In fact, they mostly got the easy stuff. So once you identify a known gold-mining district, you should be able to go out there and come back with at least small showings of flour gold.

Granite is a common rock found in most areas of North America. It can be carved and formed into exquisite countertops and comes in a wide variety of colors including red, yellow, tan, and brown. Color, composition, and patterns are all important for slabbing granite. It boasts strength and permanence and is not prone to scratching, burning, or chipping. Granite tiles find their way into stairways and even exterior building material. You can find more information at Global Granite and Tile, among other sites. Their address is www.globalgranite.com.

Gypsum is the defining mineral for 2 on the Mohs scale, so all rockhounds should have a piece of gypsum crystal in their hardness kit. A key element in plaster of paris, gypsum is also a key component of drywall, is used as a chemical binder, and even has medicinal uses. The term *alabaster* refers to white forms of both calcite and gypsum, with the term using relevance for gypsum. Common gypsum deposits in several states and provinces of North America supply sulfate fertilizers. Crystals are collectable and make interesting display pieces. The original term for gypsum means "spear stone," and spar is a name that still sticks to some varieties. Desert roses, usually crystalline gypsum embedded with sand grains, make interesting novelty items. Fibrous selenite is a common mineral. Selenite crystals in the Spear of Caves in Chihuahua, Mexico, reach 4 feet in diameter and 50 feet long. New Mexico's famed White Sands National Monument "Sands" comprise small white gypsum fragments.

Halite is common rock salt. It is not a grand addition to a mineral collection, but you can seek out a few different specimens. Slabs of colored halite, particularly from the Himalayas, make an interesting culinary addition; chefs mount raw tomato slides that pick up the salt flavor. Pure halite crystals are common in the arid Western states, such as around Utah's Great Salt Lake. One interesting display piece you can look for is a branch or piece of driftwood that's been encrusted with salt crystals over a great length of time.

Hematite is a common form of iron oxide, noted for a deep red streak even when found in its black, shiny steel-gray, or brownish state. One of the few minerals that sometimes display a botryoidal habit, hematite earned the name "kidney stone" for the bubbly, roundish form. Red hematite is the source mineral for much of the iron ore mined in Minnesota's famed Mesabi Iron Range; it gives Mars its red color as well. Red, powdery ochre is another form of hematite.

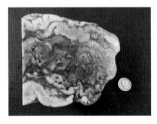

Jade comes in two varieties, and both are metamorphic rocks of superior strength: Jadeite, a pyroxene, is about 6 to 7 on the Mohs scale; the slightly softer nephrite, an amphibole, is around 6.5 on the Mohs scale. Long carved by native artisans into statues, jewelry, and weapons, jade's use dates to prehistoric times. Jadeite tends to occur in shades of bright green, brown, lavender, orange, and pink. Nephrite is usually darker, but fine white nephrite commands high prices. Nephrite sometimes displays a botryoidal, or bubbly, surface, which also aids in identification.

There are only about twelve jadeite locales around the world; one famed North America site is in Guatemala's Motagua River Valley. Other jadeite locales include California's San Benito County, the border of Mendocino and Trinity Counties, and San Luis Obispo Country.

Nephrite is slightly more abundant, with excellent deposits at Jade Mountain, Alaska; near Lander, Wyoming; near Oso, Washington; near Happy Camp and at Jade Cove, California; and along the upper Fraser River in British Columbia. Here is a link to an excellent jadeite resource: www.cigem.ca/431.html. Another good resource is *Jade Fever: Hunting the Stone of Heaven* by Stan Leaming and Rick Hudson.

Jasper is common in many creek and river gravels and in beach deposits, as it is hard and not prone to erosion. Red and tan jaspers are the most common. Most Western states have good jasper locales; the Oregon-Idaho border area contains Owyhee picture jasper, a prized, gem-quality variety. Hans Gama operates a popular website (www.worldofjaspers.com/index.html) promoting his book, *Picture Jaspers,* which has exquisite photographs of many varieties of picture jasper. Note that jaspers with a porous surface will not take a good polish.

At the far end of the metamorphic scale, **kyanite** schists denote severe heat and pressure conditions. Kyanite also shows up in gneiss, pegmatite, and quartz veins. Kyanite crystals are usually bladed or in columns that are light blue and crumbly. Blue is by far the most common color, but kyanite also appear as striking gem-quality crystals in shades of white, gray, green, yellow, orange, and even pink. Interestingly, kyanite has two distinct hardness readings, depending on which way you try to scratch it. Kyanite blades make attractive display pieces, but actual facetable crystals are rare. Idaho's Shoshone County has yielded kyanite crystals, and there are kyanite schists in numerous Western US states, as well as Georgia, Tennessee, New Hampshire, Ontario, Quebec, and Newfoundland.

Limestone is a catchall term for sedimentary rocks rich in calcium carbonate. It can form either as a chemical precipitate (travertine) or as piled-up grains. One interesting form of limestone is oolitic limestone, with large round grains several millimeters in diameter. Limestone and its magnesium-rich cousin, dolomite, can be distinguished using dilute acid—limestone fizzes energetically, while dolomite has to be powdered to get much of a reaction at all.

Rockhounds are often able to find nice seams of chert in limestone formations. Chert forms out of organic silica ooze and thus differs chemically from jasper. Limestone is also of great interest to fossil collectors, as the limestone grains in this sedimentary rock are often tiny diatom skeletons. Long used as a building material, limestone yields lime-rich fertilizers, serves as an aggregate, finds its way into medicines and cosmetics, and has other industrial uses. Most famed caves in the world were formed by groundwater dissolving limestone formations, and many significant oil deposits formed in limestone. Florida contains Cenozoic limestone deposits formed primarily from corals, while New York's Niagara Escarpment dates to the Silurian age.

Marble is a metamorphosed limestone or dolomite that has hardened significantly; it can be quite striking when solid, vivid white. Many famed buildings attest to marble's durability and beauty, including the Taj Mahal in India. Well-known marble statues include Abraham Lincoln at the Lincoln Memorial, the *Venus de Milo,* and Michelangelo's *David.* Noted US deposits include quarries in Pickens County, Georgia; Talladega County, Alabama; and in Tennessee, Vermont, and Colorado. Yule marble from Marble, Colorado, graces the Lincoln Memorial and the Tomb of the Unknown Solider and is composed of approximately 99.5 percent pure calcite.

Hunting for **meteorites** has always been a very narrow offshoot of rockhounding and gold prospecting. "Stardust"—tiny fragments of nickel-iron meteorites—makes up a small but constant portion of the black sands you collect while dredging and sluicing. Smart operators know to keep a lookout for big, chunky rocks that are inordinately heavy. Rockhounds out in the arid deserts also keep an eye out for meteorites.

Stony **Iron**
Meteorite fragment
ahara Desert, Morocco

Iron Nickel
Meteorite Fragment
Campo del Cielo
Argentina

Iron Nickel
Meteorite Fragment
Sikhote-Alin
Siberia, Russia

For old-school hunters with a practiced eye, the black fusion crust of a recent strike will stand out against white desert sand. And because most meteorites stick to a magnet, hunters can search armed only with a strong magnet on a stick.

Another way that rockhounds and gold prospectors "intersect" at meteorite hunting is in the use of metal detectors. The nickel content of iron meteorites is a dead giveaway—terrestrial rocks do not have that much nickel. Therefore, a metal detector comes in handy for nugget hunting as well as meteorite hunting. In addition, because some meteorites that reach the Earth's surface are large, detectorists have learned to create large grids that can penetrate 10 feet or more underneath a Kansas cornfield and find incredibly valuable material.

The recent popularity of the TV show *Meteorite Men* has sparked an upsurge in meteorite hunting. The show's website (www.meteoritemen .com) has material and books for sale, hints on which metal detector to purchase, and links to other informative pages. It is a great place to start.

Obsidian is a form of common rhyolite, or lava, that literally froze, or chilled, in place rather than slowly cooling. When molten rocks cool slowly, about a degree or two every hundred years, crystals tend to grow into large sheets, plates, and blades. When rocks cool faster than that, the resulting texture may be coarse polka dots or smaller, with no discernible crystals. However, when molten rhyolite chills quickly, it literally freezes into a glass, known to rockhounds as obsidian. With no crystal structure, obsidian chips into consistent conchoidal fracture patterns that aboriginals quickly learned to take advantage of, knapping arrowheads, spear points, and jewelry.

The most common form of obsidian is a jet black, but there are countless other varieties, including green, sheen, copper, root beer, mahogany, rainbow, and aurora borealis. Many Western volcanoes host obsidian deposits, including Newberry Crater National Monument, where collecting is not allowed, and at Yellowstone National Park, also off-limits. Fortunately, two popular free collecting areas do exist: Glass Buttes, between Bend and Burns in Oregon, has many different varieties of obsidian; the material at Davis Creek, in Northern California, fractures into rare "needles" that are highly prized by lapidarists for fashioning into wind chimes and other ornaments.

Common **opal** is a widespread cryptocrystalline variety of quartz; the difference from agate and jasper is that opal contains "n" molecules (where you can substitute different numbers for "n") of H_2O in its structure. The water gives opal a waxy luster but also can result in

spectacular plays of light. Spencer Opal in Idaho is a particularly noteworthy fee-dig. Another variety of precious opal occurs in petrified wood, found principally at Virgin Valley in northern Nevada. The Royal Peacock Mine is a great example; check it out at www.royalpeacock.com.

Petrified wood is not an actual geology term. "Petrified" means something turned to rock, and that is true for any tree trunk, limb, or root that has had its minerals replaced by quartz or silica. The term applies whether the wood is opalized, silicified, or

otherwise hardened. The entire process apparently occurs underground and is geologically rapid—perhaps on a scale of one hundred years. Various metallic impurities provide the vivid colors that, combined with its ability to take a polish, make petrified wood highly collectible. Large petrified logs that yield perfectly round slices and display the tree's cell structure are especially valuable.

Several parks and museums organized around significant petrified wood locales have their own web pages. Famous North America locales include the Alberta badlands and Axel Heiberg Island (Nunavut) in Canada; Ginkgo/Wanapum State Park, Washington; Petrified Forest National Park, Arizona; Gilboa Fossil Forest, New York; and Escalante Petrified Forest State Park, Utah.

Platinum weighs in at about 21.5 grams per cubic centimeter, making it heavier than gold. Platinum was an unknown noble metal until 1557. In its pure form, platinum is a beautiful white-silver metal. It is usually present in trace amounts in black sands, combined with other rare earth elements such as iridium, and it can form attractive nuggets. Early miners did not know platinum's value and apparently discarded sizable masses. Platinum has many uses in jewelry manufacture, as it resists oxidation and corrosion even at high temperature.

At the Sudbury Basin in Ontario, Canada, miners extract platinum thought to be extraterrestrial in nature, mixed with copper and nickel. The Stillwater Complex in Montana is smaller but similar in chemistry to South Africa's famed Merensky Reef, long the world's biggest source of platinum. There is a large, active alluvial platinum mine at Platinum, Alaska, where miners concentrate rich black sands. Other Western locales include near Douglas City on the Trinity River, and along Josephine Creek in southwest Oregon. Many ocean beaches along the northern Pacific coast contain significant ratios of platinum, palladium, iridium, and other rare earth elements in the black sands.

Pyrite, or "fool's gold," is one of the most versatile minerals. You can find it in the form of flattened, striated "dollars," as perfect cubes, as twelve-sided dodecahedrons, in bunches of crystals with or without other minerals, in massive zones, and replacing fossils. You can hunt for pyrite in igneous, sedimentary, or metamorphic rocks. Many mining districts in North America had pyrite showings in some form, and it is common in hard-rock tailings where sulfides were common.

Ancient firearms used pyrite and steel to create reliable sparks. Despite the derogatory term *fool's gold,* there is a catch. Chalcopyrite contains a little copper and can lead to bornite, a notable copper ore. When pyrite teams with arsenic in its crystal structure, the result is arsenopyrite. Nevada's Carlin Trend is a massive disseminated gold deposit in sedimentary rock shot through with pyrite and arsenopyrite. Most of the specimen-quality pyrite on the market today comes from San Jose de Huanzala Mine in Peru. Hardin County, Illinois, has a long history of producing excellent pyrite specimens; Illinois and Arizona contain deposits of pyrite "dollars." Spain seems to contain the majority of museum-quality pyrite cubes, but one notable exception is Spruce Ridge at Snoqualmie Pass, Washington, which is famed for striking cubes nestled into quartz scepters.

Quartz comes in many varieties and colors. Clear, perfectly terminated crystalline quartz is highly collectible. Smoky quartz is gray to jet black, and thanks to its location near old, degrading granite, faced considerable radiation. Amethyst, an attractive violet or purple, owes its color to trace elements, especially iron, and irradiation.

One classic place to collect perfect quartz crystals is at the Herkimer fee-dig operation in upper New York. Here is a website to get you started at the Crystal Grove Diamond Mine and Campground: www.crystal grove.com. Amethyst is common in North America; the largest amethyst mine is said to be at Thunder Bay, Ontario. Most big, showy amethyst vugs with spectacular crystals come from Brazil. Smoky quartz is also common; some notable deposits are in the Black Hills of South Dakota, the Sawtooth Mountains of Idaho, and various districts in Colorado. A free collecting area at Lolo Pass, on the Idaho-Montana border, attracts collectors year after year.

Sapphire is a variant on corundum, with a simple chemical formula of Al_2O_3. Sapphire comes in every color except red; red sapphires are rubies. Minute contamination by elements such as copper, iron, or magnesium, among others, accounts for the different colors, but all forms are chemically the same. Being very hard, sapphires mostly occur in alluvial or placer deposits, since they resist erosion. Miners also dig sapphires from igneous and metamorphic rocks, but not often. Montana has at least three locales that yield alluvial sapphires: Yogo Gulch, west of Lewiston; Rock Creek, near Phillipsburg, and Spokane Bar on the Mis-

souri River, near Helena. Here are a couple good websites to get you started: www.sapphire mining.com and www .sapphire mine.com. There are numerous YouTube videos about Montana sapphire fee-dig operations.

Silver ore deposits are often not particularly collectible—tetrahedrite is a major ore, and it is usually a heavy, dull black rock. In rich silver deposits, miners find native silver in ornate, comb-like forms that resemble horns—hence the name, horn silver. Most prospectors locate silver ore as a by-product in their search for gold. Nevada, Arizona, and New Mexico contain specimen silver deposits, while the vast silver deposits of Idaho's Silver Valley are not noted for specimens.

Soapstone is a soft metamorphic rock, usually green, tan, brown, or yellow. For thousands of years artisans have fashioned soapstone into ornaments, fetishes, jewelry, and sculptures. The mineral names include steatite and pyrophyllite, but the term *soapstone* applies to any rock that is rich in talc and has a soft, soapy feel. Soapstone has talc and asbestos in abundance, and while hardness increases as harder minerals show up, the material is usually so soft you can carve it with a fingernail. Even a simple set of files, saws, and different grades of sandpaper will yield a nice art piece. Native Americans fashioned soapstone into pipes for smoking various herbs; the most popular use today is for countertops. Soapstone is common around schists and low-grade metamorphic terrains. Soapstone deposits are found in many areas of North American, including Georgia, Ohio, Washington, Oregon, California, and British Columbia.

Staurolite represents very high-grade metamorphism and is associated with staurolite schist. Although it usually presents in a long, brown, tabular habit, staurolite can show up as twinned crystals forming *X*'s and crosses as well as cubes, which are highly collectible (if not particularly valuable). They make interesting display pieces and jewelry. Staurolite is the state mineral of Georgia, but the most famed locale is Fairy Stone State Park in Virginia. Minnesota, New Mexico, and northern Idaho also host good staurolite crystal collecting locales.

Sunstone (also called andesine) is a member of the feldspar family. Sunstones are associated with basalt flows and often occupy voids, vugs, and air pockets near the top of the flow. Typically straw yellow in color, common sunstones look like liquid drops of honey when polished. Less-common varieties of sunstone contain impurities such as copper. The term *schiller* refers to the effect of turning different colors as the stone rotates in the light. Some recent cinder cones in Idaho contain small crystals. Sunstone is Oregon's state mineral, and the Rabbit Hills contain both fee-dig operations and a free collecting area. Two websites to get you started are for the Dust Devil Mine (www.dustdevilmining.com) and the Spectrum Mine (www.high desertgemsandminerals.com/html/spectrum_sunstone_mines.html).

Thundereggs are the state rock of Oregon. These small, crystal-filled geodes originate in rhyolite flows. (Nature of the Northwest has an interesting write-up at www.naturenw.org/rock-thundereggs.htm.) The interior of thundereggs sometimes contains agate, chalcedony, quartz crystals, calcite, or carnelian, usually in the rough shape of a star. Numerous patterns, shapes, and forms are revealed when thundereggs are sawed in half and the cut polished. The most famous thunderegg beds are at Oregon's Richardson Rock Ranch (http://richardsonrockranch.com). There are estimates that 60 percent of the world's thundereggs originated at the ranch, but many Western states host thunderegg beds, including California, Nevada, and Idaho.

Topaz sits at 8 on the Mohs scale. It is a great addition to any mineral collection, if for no other reason than its inclusion in your personal Mohs kit, where it fits between corundum (9) and quartz (7). Topaz crystals are orthorhombic and are typically colorless, but they can be light gray, slightly yellow, or even light blue and pink as they near gem quality. Topaz is an aluminum silicate, with fluorine inserted into the crystal lattice; in rare instances it forms in granite pegmatites and certain rhyolites. Gem-quality topaz is highly prized for jewelry, fashioned into faceted stones for pendants, rings, and earrings. There are minor deposits in Texas, but the classic North American topaz-collecting locale is at Topaz Mountain, Utah. Here is a website to get you started: http://publiclands.org/explore/site.php?id=1276.

Tourmaline comes in at least three varieties. The most common is black schorl, which is about 99 percent of all tourmaline. Dravite, which is dark yellow, is primarily European. That leaves elbaite, also first known in Europe, which comes in a variety of colors—red, pink, green, blue, and clear. Tourmalines from Maine vary from raspberry pink to minty green.

Small schorl crystals associated with muscovite schist are common at Mica Mountain in Idaho. Larger schorl specimens are common in most pegmatites, including large deposits in the Black Hills of the Dakotas. The Himalaya Mine and surrounding deposits in San Diego County, California, supply most of the elbaite tourmaline on the market today. Their website is www.highdesertgemsandminerals.com/html/himalaya_mine_digs.html.

Turquoise is a prized North American gemstone, with a characteristic blue-green color that looks especially attractive when set in silver. It occurs as vein fillings and in seams but also forms as small nuggets. Iran and the Sinai Peninsula are historically important production centers, but there are many North American deposits of note. Since copper is one of its principal components, turquoise is associated with the copper-producing locales of Arizona, New Mexico, and Nevada. California and Colorado also host significant turquoise deposits.

Zeolites are a strange, relatively unexplored category of silicates that defy easy description. Quite common, they are found in cracks and vugs in volcanic rocks, or where volcanic rocks and ash beds withstand a

persistent flush of alkali groundwater. Zeolites are ringed silicates, and their porous structure makes them useful for absorbents and filters—for example, in cat litter.

Mineralogists and crystal hunters know that zeolites probably offer one of the best chances to name a new mineral, as there are almost infinite varieties out there. The definitive "bible" for zeolite information is *Zeolites of the World* by Rudy Tschernich. Long out of print, it is available for download from the Minerals Database at www.mindat .org/article.php/507/Mindat%27s+15th+Birthday+and+a+present+for+ everyone.

GATOR GIRL'S BEST ADVICE EVER

Now that you have zeroed in on something to look for, you can start to concentrate on researching where to go. Before going any further, here is some advice from "Gator Girl" about improving your rockhounding experience. This advice also applies to pretty rocks, gold, fossils, and meteorites; check it out at www.gatorgirlrocks.com/resources/the-best-ever-tips-for-a.html. It is paraphrased below for immediate field application.

- **Join a local club.** Get in-person networking, information sharing, and more by hooking up with a club, council, federation, or similar group. Set yourself up to talk regularly with like-minded people who have probably found what you are interested in and have most likely already been to the places you want to visit. Get involved, go to meetings, and, if the club isn't already doing so, push for sponsored field trips led by knowledgeable experts. An up-to-date list of clubs for rocks, gems, lapidary, and fossil digging is available at www.rockhounds.com/rockshop/clublist .shtml.
- **Know the state fossil.** Or state rock, or state gem. If it's important enough to represent the entire state, it must be significant. And something that significant should not be too hard to find in the field. Check www.nature.nps.gov/geology/nationalfossilday/state_ fossils.cfm for a list of official state fossils.
- **Visit museums.** Local museums should have displays of significant specimens from the area. They also often have great

shops for purchasing books and more. Museums might just be small hole-in-the-wall setups or huge, like the Smithsonian in Washington, D.C., or the American Museum of Natural History in New York City. Regardless, you owe it to yourself to see what their curator has deemed important.

- **Go to shows.** Groups put a lot of energy and effort into organizing annual rock, gem, and fossil shows. These are significant social networking opportunities and include top professionals, vendors, and dealers. Some of these folks travel from show to show, and they know what you want—and what questions you are dying to ask. Other experts might use that one show as their big event of the year. You can tour the booths, check out the displays, strike up conversations, pick up new books and tools, and spend a little money on your favorite hobby. *Rock & Gem* magazine keeps a list of top shows here: www.rockngem .com/show-dates-display/?ShowState=ALL.

- **Visit shops.** Never pass up a local rock and gem shop! And don't be afraid to call shops, either. Local shops are typically run by dedicated expert rockhounds who know all the top collecting places and like-minded people in that area. They can steer you away from areas depleted over time or with access issues, and they usually have good prices on tools and equipment. Spend a little time and money, and you'll find your visit well worth it. These folks are a dying breed. There used to be shops in every significant rockhounding region. Now there are more shops online. Pebble Pup (http://pebblepup.com) has a link to gem shops in most Western states.

- **Stop at historic sites.** Always stop at parks and monuments devoted to mining, milling, dredging, or digging for gold and minerals. If there is a park for a meteorite or a fossil, you should visit just to get some good pictures. For a list of national parks and monuments with a geology theme, visit www.cr.nps.gov/ history/online_books/geology/geology.pdf.

- **Go to the library.** Your local library is a valuable resource. Talk to the reference librarian about your needs, and enlist help tracking down those obscure reports and maps. The Gemological Institute of America has a fantastic library to visit in person as well as online at www.gia.edu/research-resources/library/index .html.

- **Check with the state.** The USGS is great, but so are the state-run departments, and they usually have much better specific information on local districts, fossil sites, etc. Here's an interactive map that will deliver you to each state's geology resource: www.stategeologists.org.
- **Visit universities.** Never pass up the opportunity to visit the natural history museum of a local university. Even better are notable institutions such as the Colorado School of Mines (www.mines.edu).
- **Protect your eyes.** Gator Girl says you should never buy a rock hammer until you have the safety goggles in place FIRST. If you've ever heard a piece of rock go whizzing past your ear, you'll understand this final piece of advice

CHAPTER 2
WHERE TO FIND IT

Collectors generally face two dilemmas in their quest for interesting collectibles:

1. **Specific goal.** Where can I go to collect that **one certain collectible** I am interested in?

2. **Specific area.** What general opportunities exist in that **one certain area** I intend to visit?

In the first case, you want to learn everything you can about that one collectible. You want to know what the material looks like, where collectors have found it in the past, and what kind of equipment you need. If possible, you want to find someone who has been to an area and can give you a firsthand report. If a rock club or prospecting club is planning a trip for that material, you want to know that schedule.

In the second case, you want to learn everything you can about a specific area to ensure that you do not go looking for one thing only to find out later that everyone else goes there for something completely different. You will probably need to go into some detail about the geologic setting in order to get a framework for what is possible to find there. You also want to be sure you have the right equipment.

In many ways, the *goal* and *area* scenarios overlap. You need the same camping gear and the same equipment; you face the same transportation challenges, which we will talk about later. Your research challenges are actually quite similar. In both cases you can use many modern tools that simply did not exist years ago to dramatically increase your odds of success.

First let's look at some of the tried-and-true resources that have served collectors so well through the years and see how things have progressed.

OLD-SCHOOL REFERENCE MATERIALS

We have come a long way from scraps of paper with "*X* marks the spot," but for decades printed books were the best resource available. Many of them are still useful when researching, so let's take a quick look at these resources.

Earth Treasures

One of the most complete listings of collecting locales is also one of the most frustrating: the *Earth Treasures* series. Allan W. Eckert compiled the series in the 1970s. He divided the United States into four quadrants, so you need four books to build a complete set. You can pick up old copies for a good price—usually less than $10 each.

To its credit, the *Earth Treasures* series lists around 5,000 rock, gem, fossil, and gold prospecting locales. It is an excellent general resource but far from complete. The directions are often out of date, with road names and numbers changed or routes diverted. That is not the author's fault—things change in forty years. The main problem is that there is no real explanation in the introduction about the source material for the listings, so readers are left to wonder how much is based on discussions with old-timers and how much is just plain hearsay.

Many fee-dig operations listed in the book are now closed, either depleted of material or no longer kept up as farms and ranches get handed down to the next generation. In some places, however, the information is as good and accurate now as it was back in the day. Consider these books as a nice starting list for where material was historically available, and understand that many areas have since closed because of road construction, new malls and subdivisions, dams and reservoirs, etc. Fortunately, each volume contains an index, so if you are interested in a certain locale or a certain material, you should be able to track down potential areas to spur further research.

Western Gem Hunters Atlas

The *Western Gem Hunters Atlas*, written by Cyril Johnson, is copyrighted 1994, but by 1998 was in its twenty-eighth edition, so the oldest information probably dates to 1970. This guide is easy to use and consistently accurate, and it rarely leads to wild-goose chases. It is sometimes a bit vague and may use older names for material or geographical features. There are no GPS coordinates, and once you leave the highway, road names are nonexistent. Still, it is a must-have for rockhounds who frequently travel across the western United States.

Here is a snip from the foreword (p.2), which explains their motivation and dedication:

> Over a period of years we have noted and compiled every gem location made known to us. Many of the localities shown on these maps have been publicized before, and some have been worked over quite thoroughly. However, most new finds are made in the same general areas. We just have to search a little further or dig a little deeper. . . . This little atlas cannot pretend to replace the wealth of material contained in the mineral magazines and Gem Trail books. The serious rock collector will want to supplement with detailed information.

You can also find Cy Johnson's *Coast to Coast Gem Atlas* and Robert Johnson's *N.W. Gem Fields and Ghost Towns Atlas,* covering different geographies.

Gold Diggers Atlas

For beginning gold panners, there are few resources like the *Gold Diggers Atlas*. Written by Robert Neil Johnson in 1971, it is a handy reference; and while it covers only the Western states, it covers them well. This consistently reliable book lists old districts by their old name and shows legendary ghost towns and lost treasure information when applicable. Its road mileages are not always accurate, as events have overtaken many highway junctions, but you can usually get a good idea of how to reach historic mines. The best way to use this book is to consider it as a beginning data point and then track down the relevant USGS documents or old state geology bulletins to help home in on the actual location.

USGS Professional Bulletin 610

The best reference on American gold mining is USGS Professional Bulletin 610, "Principal Gold Producing Districts of the United States." For years this out-of-print document was difficult to find, but a PDF is now available on the Arizona Geological Survey page at http://mines .az.gov/DigitalLibrary/USGS-PP. Published in 1968, the document could use an update, but it is a must-have for any serious prospector. It lists all the important gold mining districts for twenty-one states and is a scrupulously researched starting point for the geological papers and reports for those areas. (If you are researching Canada, Australia, or South America, you should be able to find an equivalent book from the respective federal geology agency.)

As an example, the figure below shows a sample map for the gold mining districts of South Dakota. While you might be satisfied at first to consider everything there as part of the Black Hills, geologists have gone into much more detail. Each mining district gets a more-exact recap later on, with production figures, important geology, and specific references. Armed with that knowledge, you can track down key reports that often contain detailed maps and even more geology details. If you find the right documents, you will know exactly what ores the miners extracted and how interesting the tailings might be for exotic minerals.

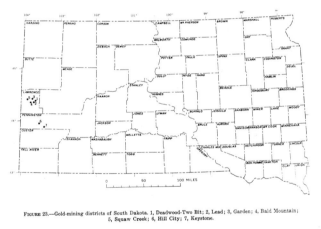

FIGURE 23.—Gold-mining districts of South Dakota. 1, Deadwood-Two Bit; 2, Lead; 3, Garden; 4, Bald Mountain; 5, Squaw Creek; 6, Hill City; 7, Keystone.

Sample USGS map for South Dakota gold mining districts

FalconGuides

Rockhounds have long relied on field guides to aid them in their expeditions. There are FalconGuides for just about every Western state, and you should always pick one up when there is coverage for a region you're about to visit. The newer guides include GPS coordinates and excellent updated information. You can purchase via Amazon or your local bookstore. Visit the publisher at www.falcon.com.

Gem Guides

Like Falcon, the Gem Guides folks have developed an extensive offering of state-by-state rockhounding guides. Most of their guides are up to date and include GPS coordinates. Older titles also cover multi-state areas such as the Midwest, based on the pioneering work of June Culp Zeitner, but they lack GPS information and are due for an update. Check out the full list at www.gemguidesbooks.com.

Other Printed Materials

There are many other books and materials out there worth adding to your personal library. For years various rockhounds with a penchant for writing have compiled small pamphlets and booklets about their favorite areas, and many of these are still available, even though out of print.

Consider *Rockhounding Out of Bishop, California* (1967) by Cora B. Houghtaling. This book is an excellent example of the fine work done by our rockhounding predecessors. The following sample paragraph about the Phantom Hill area provides a good reason to trust whatever the writer says—and wish she had written a lot more books:

> That was a hill that was hard to give up. We returned day after day, each day finding another good reason for returning. Finally, when we had exhausted our good reasons for returning, we said 'Good-bye Phantom Hill' and headed for home. We were driving along in silence when my husband said, 'Well, we will have to go back tomorrow. I left my tools in a hole.' Then we all talked at once . . . so happy to have an excuse for returning." (p. 23)

Limits of Printed Books

Just to reinforce why you have it so good as a modern rockhound and prospector, let's use an example to show how far things have come. Consider the printed literature for Glass Buttes, Oregon, one of the premier free obsidian collecting locales in the world.

The *Earth Treasures* series list the Glass Buttes locale as follows: "Bend area: southeast on US-20 to MM-79; turn right on old road to Glass Buttes. Obsidian: many colors; fair quality (on surface) to highest quality (needing to be removed from matrix)."

The accompanying map is worthless, as it points to downtown Bend, while the locale is about 80 miles to the east. You get a good idea of what is collectible, but there are few details for further planning other than finding the general locale of that milepost for a right turn of unknown duration.

The *Western Gem Hunters Atlas* has a lot more detail. Now you know your turn is a certain mileage from two points and that you're searching a wide area for a couple of interesting varieties of obsidian. However, there are still no mileages into the collecting area, much less for the unique varieties.

James Mitchell did a decent job of detailing roads and locales in *Gem Trails of Oregon* (1990). You can find the turn from the highway, and you get a better idea of distances on those back roads. He shows multiple collecting locales, with great variety.

Tim Fisher of www.orerockon .com has overlaid about thirty key spots at Glass Buttes onto a general topographic map. The detailed map (not shown) is even better,

2010 Overview map of Glass Buttes from Tim Fisher's Ore-Rock-On DVD

and there are accompanying GPS coordinates for each site. Fisher was critical of previous maps, and he obviously improved on them greatly. Fisher's Ore-Rock-On DVD has more than 2,700 GPS listings for Oregon, Washington, and Idaho, covering rock, gem, and fossil collecting locales.

Always consider print sources for historic collecting areas as a starting point. Then use your web resources, phone calls to government agencies, and other data to firm up your plans. Chances are good that you might hear of a place for the first time in an old printed document, so what follows are some good online sources for picking up print material.

ONLINE RESOURCES

Books
You probably do not need much help in finding an old book nowadays; just about every bibliophile has an account on www.Amazon.com. Some vendors specializing in rock, gem, and gold prospecting titles are listed below.

Bob's Rock Shop
www.rockhounds.com/rockshop/books/collecting.shtml

This site has extensive listings in many different fields, including lapidary, wire wrapping, casting, faceting, chain making, and stone setting. The "Smithing" section alone includes titles on engraving, goldsmithing, patinas, knife making, creating metal beads, and much more.

Rocks and Gems

www.rocksandgems.info/books/books_collecting_guides.shtml

This site offers an extensive inventory of books concerning rock and mineral collection, lapidary, gold prospecting, treasure hunting, videos, and more.

Book Finder

www.bookfinder4u.com/search_6/Rock_and_Gem.html

Book finder aggregates the online listings for over 130 resources, so it has quite a reach and lists hundreds of titles.

Powell's Books

www.powells.com

The charm of this store in Portland, Oregon, is its used-book offerings. Out-of-print books tend to be hard to find, but over many years this store has maintained a reputation for book buying that sustains its used-book titles while offering plenty of new books too.

ROCK AND GEM RESOURCES

The Internet continues to host more and more comprehensive online locale guides for collectors of all types. While these compilations are a great service, keep in mind that the list authors rarely spend time checking or verifying locales.

Beste's Rock and Gem Location Guide

www.missourigeologists.org/Min-Loc1-2005.pdf

Originally published in print, this three-volume set of PDFs (change "Min-Loc1" to "Min-Loc2" and "Min-Loc3" to get all three files) is titled *A Location Guide for Rock Hounds in the United States*. It's available from the Association of Missouri Geologists; author Robert C. Beste is a professional geologist by training. He has not visited every single locale, but he tried.

Here's a snip from his preface:

Each year I vacation in the field, collecting gem and mineral samples somewhere in the United States or Canada, and each year I spend hours looking through reference materials to plot out my trip (to include locations which interest me). Last year as I started this annual process, I decided to find a new and more complete reference to reduce my research time. To my dismay, there were some new references for individual states, but the most useful references were no longer in print and were rarely available to collectors at local libraries outside of USGS repositories. This prompted me to collect all my books and personal references, along with many trips to the reference library, and try to put together a useful tool for some of my friends. It should be said that my personal contribution, outside of editing, was only about 1% of this effort. . . . This is by no means a complete end all reference and some of the references are more of historical value for new exploration than anything else, but there is enough information to be useful to most gem and mineral collectors." (p. v)

Northwest Obsidian Studies Lab
www.obsidianlab.com

This team is in Corvallis, Oregon, and has developed spectrographic methods for analyzing obsidian artifacts and cross-referencing the material back to its source locale. By doing so they have created fascinating models for the spread of source obsidian from key deposits in Oregon, Idaho, and Wyoming. Their "Northwest Research Obsidian Studies Lab Source Catalog" is an interactive map of the western United States and, when possible, contains links to studies for more information. There are further links to state-by-state source maps, but actual GPS coordinates or additional locale details are rare.

Quarries
http://quarriesandbeyond.org/site_map.html

Abandoned quarries are often excellent collecting locales when all the legal restrictions are lifted. The decorative stone industry has existed for centuries selling high-quality granite, diorite, and marble slabs and blocks. Limestone quarries often contain collectible fossils, and basalt quarries can host zeolite vugs and veins. Abandoned sand and gravel pits might offer possibilities for agate picking or other tumbler material.

This website is produced by Peggy B. Perazzo, historical dealer of stone and finished products, and contains information about noted quarries plus good links to state geology resources.

Obey all NO TRESPASSING signs, and respect the rights of landowners. If there are signs with contact information, use them as an opportunity to learn if there are any interesting specimens left at the site, if there are other opportunities open to the public, or if you can purchase material.

FOSSIL COLLECTING RESOURCES

Because of the complicated legal restrictions in place concerning vertebrate fossil collecting, lists such as these are rare. As more master's theses and doctoral dissertations come online, these databases should grow in content, accuracy, and completeness. For now, you mostly get general information on a state-by-state basis.

Fossil Sites

http://fossilsites.com/index.html

This ambitious site has existed for many years, dedicated to listing fossil collecting locales across the United States and Canada. Some of the material is doubtful, some is misleading, and some is spot-on. All of that is spelled out in the large disclaimer and information page, some of which is included here:

> There are plenty of errors in the list. Some of the original material was incorrect or ambiguous. Errors were made transcribing some of it to index cards decades ago, and more errors transcribing that into the computer more recently. It has been spell checked, and checked for plausibility. Some of the hopeless material was deleted. In general, anything was kept that looked like it might be remotely useful to someone someday. Many of the sites are closed to collecting or buried under shopping centers, highways, or housing developments. Closed sites will stay on the list, as they are sometimes reopened, and sometimes the same rocks and fossils will turn up 100 yards or 100 miles down the road. . . . Some of the sites listed probably never existed in the first place, and other sites have been developed over and/or reclaimed out of existence. Many of the localities when found will be closed to fossil

collecting, and of those that are not, many will prove to be unproductive. A few of the sites are accessible to large groups without special arrangements.

Fossil Guy
www.fossilguy.com/sites/index.htm
This is an excellent recap of top spots in Ohio, West Virginia, and nearby locales.

Fossil Facts and Finds
www.fossils-facts-and-finds.com/fossil_hunting_usa.html
This is a great starting point to identify areas near you that contain fossils.

Texas Paleo
www.texaspaleo.com/usmaps/paleosites.html
This growing list shows some promise.

Fossiel.Net
http://english.fossiel.net/locations/locations.php#land
This site is not exhaustive, but it is international in scope and seems to be growing.

ONLINE GOLD REPORTS
Modern prospectors are getting better about sharing their locale information. There are two in particular that contain good historical information.

Iowa Gold
www.iowagold.com/WHERE_TO_FIND_GOLD_USA_PAGES/where_to_find_gold_usa.htm
Iowa Gold lists locales by state and county.

DIY Plans
www.gpex.ca/homemade-gold-prospecting-tools.html
This site has multiple plans and instructions for various gold mining and gold recovery contraptions. You might see something you like, or you might be inspired to create something revolutionary.

ONLINE METEORITE LOCALES

Meteorite hunters sit at the top of the food chain when it comes to using modern tools. They rely on metal detectors, they create excellent maps, and their discoveries rely on detailed lab analysis for confirmation and identification.

The Meteorological Society

www.lpi.usra.edu/meteor/metbull.php

This is a key meteorite web page that you should bookmark. They have built an extensive database of discoveries, and you can export their data into Google Earth. You can search the database in multiple ways depending, for example, on whether you are looking for sites with tons of material collected or a certain type of rare meteorite, such as pallasites.

Washington University (St. Louis)

http://meteorites.wustl.edu/numbers_by_state.htm

Randy Korotev compiled a map to show known meteorite discoveries in the United States based on the Meteorological Society's data. He has some interesting graphs that show the number of falls per year, average, and size of the falls.

APPS

One of the great advances since the iPhone and iPad became popular has been the explosion of "apps" for users. Short for "applications," apps are usually small, focused, single-purpose software tools that typically are free or low cost. The best news you can now hear about software you're looking for is the phrase, "Yeah, there's an app for that."

Rock and Gem Apps

We talked about general geology apps in chapter 1. The apps here focus on where to find and how to identify material. Note that this is a growing field for both Apple and Android devices, and the products listed here may not be around when you check, or may be superseded by something better. Think of these as a starting point.

Gems and Minerals

This pictorial database of common gems and minerals contains excellent high-resolution images of several hundred minerals and is priced at only $1. The author included informative text and a nice set of features to manipulate the data. It's not a key—you cannot search by individual properties.

Rocks & Minerals
Oriented more toward kids, this app covers all the basic facts that elementary and middle school kids need to know about the rock cycle, different types of rocks and minerals, and their properties and uses. It covers igneous, sedimentary, and metamorphic rocks, with many examples in each type. It's limited in scope but worth checking out.

Rocks & Gems
Also geared toward students, this app might come in handy for high school students or college students taking mineralogy lab. It's not a replacement for the better rock and gem books, however.

Gems and Jewels
This premium app, priced at $13.99, was created by the University of Chicago Press and Touch Press in collaboration with the Chicago Field Museum. The photography is excellent, and the materials are of the highest quality. There are loads of textual information, and everything is put together nicely.

Crystal Guide Pocekt Edition
More geared toward the healing properties of gems and crystals, this guide has plenty of information and decent photography.

Minerals and Gemstones
This app is a reference guide to 300 different minerals and gemstones. Each entry includes detailed information about streak, color, luster, hardness, and specific gravity, among other details. There is also information about rock-forming processes.

Geology Mineral ID
Field work can go a lot easier with an app like this one, which lets you input up to twelve unique characteristics to identify your sample. The decent photographs allow you to pinpoint your rock or mineral with confidence, and the full mineral list is browsable. The interface is easy

Field kit for streak and hardness tests. From top clockwise: streak plate, glass (5.5), old penny (3.5), nail (7), fluorite (4), apatite (5), feldspar (6), quartz (7), and topaz (8).

to use and should make you proficient quickly. Still, it's no replacement for a kit such as shown above.

Rockhound

This is a good start on some of the well-known collecting locales, including GPS coordinates. You can add your own information to tailor the sites to your specific quest. There is also information about the tools you might need to bring.

Fossil Apps

1400+ Dinosaur Handbook Complete

Geared for beginning dinosaur hunters, this app mostly offers photographs and pictures, rather than insightful text. Over time, the quality of the photographs should improve, and there is a lot of easily available writing that could be added.

Web Vendor

Tony Funk and his wife, Chris, own and operate www.IdahoRockShop.com, a full-featured online rock shop specializing in slabs, rough, and famed Idaho materials such as Bruneau jasper and Willow Creek jasper.

I first got into rocks when I was little. My grandfather had a friend who was a rock dealer at Quartzsite; every year his friend would send me a box of rocks. I still have those boxes at my dad's house, all labeled in scribbly handwriting.

About seven or eight years ago, I broke my leg in a snowmobile accident, but I had no insurance to pay for $75 per hour PT sessions. The therapist told me to really work the leg and to build up my muscles. I had always liked going out to the desert, so I would go out three times a week and hobble around on my crutches.

One of those places I went to had lots of agates lying around on the ground. At first I came back to the pickup with a few pockets full of rocks. After a while I wired two one-gallon paint pails to my crutches. I would wander around until they were full, then go back and empty them. By the time I was finished with PT, I was wiring five-gallon buckets to my crutches and filling them up two to four times a week. When I got back, I would get online to see what I had found and ended up joining an online forum called Rocktumblinghobby. I am still an active member, and I belong to several other online rock and lapidary forums. I also belong to the Magic Valley Gem Club in Twin Falls and help with some of the field trips.

SOFTWARE, DVDS, AND OTHER TOOLS

HystWare Mines and Minerals
HystWare is a moderately priced Windows-based package that lists detailed information about abandoned mines throughout the United States. Once you know the name of a mine in a district you want to visit, you can look it up here and get much more information. This is especially valuable if the mine isn't listed on www.mindat.org, the usual place to look. For more information go to www.HystWare.com.

Ore-Rock-On
This DVD lists more than 2,700 Pacific Northwest sites of interest to rock and gem collectors and fossil hunters. Creator Tim Fisher has done an outstanding job of referencing fossil collecting locales, and he has verified an astonishing number of the listings. There are good GPS coordinates, and you can overlay them onto Google Earth for easy reference. It is well worth the price. Go to www.orerockon.com.

Rockhounds.com
Check the listings at Rockhounds.com for more information about software tools, apps, databases, and more. For example, www.rockhounds.com/rockshop/database.shtml lists several database CDs and DVDs for sale. Be prepared for some of these resources to be discontinued, but with luck they may be converted into apps in the future.

ROCK AND MINERAL WEBSITES
We've already talked about joining a club to improve your networking. One of the best parts of joining a club, whether to look for rocks and minerals, prospect for gold, dig for fossils, or search for meteorites, is when the club sponsors field trips.

Rockhound Field Trips
http://rockhound-field-trips.ning.com
If you have never been on a rockhounding trip before, you should probably start slow and first join a group of experienced rockhounds. This site covers trips for California and the southwestern United States; you will want to find a relevant link for your particular area.

Minerals Database

www.mindat.org

There are many great sources online for information about minerals. This great site has stood the test of time by continuing to expand; being full of helpful information; having a keen, scientific background; and limiting advertisers while still letting them get their message through. Every rockhound should have this site bookmarked.

Mama's Minerals

http://mamasminerals.com

This is a commercial site, but when you want to add specimens that you have no hope of collecting on your own, it's a great place to start. They have a good mailing list, with constant specials and deals.

Web Minerals

http://webmineral.com

Bookmark this wonderful, fact-filled site, and check back regularly with its "What's New?" feature. Out of 10,000 distinct minerals identified, this site is up to about 4,700.

Mineral and Gemstone Kingdom

www.minerals.net

This site isn't restricted to just minerals; you can also use it to search for information about rock specimens.

AJS Gems

www.ajsgem.com

AJS is named for Arnie J. Silverberg. He is a major worldwide importer and exporter of numerous varieties of rough and polished gemstones, including ruby, sapphire, tourmaline, spinel, topaz, and garnet, plus precious and semiprecious stones from Burma, Sri Lanka (Ceylon), Africa, Thailand, and beyond. His website has pictures, educational information, and many articles to give you more information.

All About Gemstones

Go to www.allaboutgemstones.com/mohs_hardness_scale.html for a good Mohs scale.

Rock and Mineral Apps

Billed as the home to "All Things Mineralogical Online," The Vug offers a list of free mineral and rock apps for Android phone users at www .the-vug.com/vug/qrcode-appstore.html#.UL-F4Ib5X5M. Here is a partial listing that is sure to expand:

Minerals for Sale

Reliable dealers and updated deals on minerals several times each week.

Mineral Collector's Resource

Provides easy access to several useful websites for mineral collectors.

The Arkenstone

Access to mineral specimen sales from Rob Lavinsky and The Arkenstone at www.iRocks.com.

Crocoite

Information about the historic Adelaide Mine, located near Dundas in Tasmania, world famous for its beautiful crocoite specimens.

Green Mountain Minerals

Photos by world-famous photographer Jeff Scovil of beautiful minerals and gems, such as tourmaline, aquamarine, tanzanite, cerussite, and bastnaesite.

Cinderhill

Easy access to www.cinderhill.com and its assortment of beautiful pendants, cabochons, drusy beads, unique wire-wrap necklaces, and natural mineral specimens. Look for their video guide to wire-wrap jewelry design.

Mineral Auctions

Access to www.mineralauctions.com, featuring low starting prices on gems and minerals.

Mineral and Crystal Bookstore

Easy access to www.the-vug.com, a seller of field guides, mineral magazines, books about jewelry making, and mineralogy textbooks.

Tanzanite
Detailed information about tanzanite mining.

Treasured Minerals
Twenty-five mineral photos to view or use as wallpaper, including agates, aquamarines, gold, tourmaline, garnets, and more. There is also a link to "Treasured Minerals"—a guide through the minerals of the Russ Behnke Collection, which you can view at www.russbehnke.com.

Weinrich Minerals
Mineral photos from www.WeinrichMineralsInc.com.

Fine Mineral Auctions
Access to mineral auctions from Dan & Diana Weinrich of www.Weinrich MineralsInc.com.

Crystal Classics
Access to Crystal Classic's Mineral Sales website: www.CrystalClassics .co.uk.

Kristalle
Access to minerals from the Kristalle offices of Wayne and Dona Leight.

Wolfe Lapidary Cabochons
Access to the cabochon jewelry of www.WolfeLapidary.com.

Tom Wolfe Minerals
Shortcut to www.TomWolfeMinerals.com and Wolfe's agates and petrified wood.

Mineral Classics
Access to Brian Kosnar's Mineral Classics website: www.MinClassics .com. He is an expert in minerals from Colorado and Bolivia.

Kosnar Gem Co.
Access to the fine jewelry cut and produced by Brett and Allyce Kosnar.

Mineral Collecting Los Angeles
Information about mineral collecting locations just outside Los Angeles.

Mineral Collecting Quartzite
Information about mineral collecting locations in La Paz County, Arizona.

Other Apps
Once you start loading up your iPad, iPhone, Android phone, or whatever device you use, here are some other apps to consider adding:

The Periodic Table
Detailed information about each element.

Mining Industry
Understand geology and basic mining techniques.

Multi-Protractor
Measure angles.

Multi-Measure
Convert measurements; understand Troy ounces.

Science Glossary
Understand complex words and key phrases.

Planets 2.0
Know the constellations and planets.

First Aid
Understand basic first aid.

Medical Information
Access detailed medical information beyond first aid.

Survival Tips
Survive in the woods as long as your battery holds up.

If you've made it this far, you have already greatly increased your odds for a successful expedition. By arming yourself with updated local information, including maps showing roads, landmarks, and geology, you should be able to locate the areas you want to explore.

SOCIAL NETWORKING

Thanks to the growth of the Internet, there has been a dramatic increase in the sophistication of rockhounds and gold prospectors. The public may have an outdated image of grizzled old sourdoughs who look like Yosemite Sam and wear long red underwear with big white buttons, but nothing could be further from the truth. As a group, we are wired, plugged in, and future ready. The truth is that your options for gathering useful, firsthand information have increased dramatically over the past few years, and one of the best skills you can pick up is broadly defined as social networking. Loosely put, it's your ability to find like-minded people who are interested in the same things you are interested in and then communicate, share, etc., among yourselves.

Here are some websites that you could be using to make yourself an even better electronic researcher.

Facebook

www.facebook.com

It would be great if everyone who goes out in the field searching for geologic treasure had a personal Facebook page to show off his or her newest treasures and acquisitions. This free site is generally easy to set up and maintain. You can post specimen pictures and your own collecting movies, as well as create links to articles that interest you. With a little care and feeding, your personal page soon becomes a unique place. Yes, you can play games, join causes, and otherwise spend lots of nonproductive time, but Facebook can be so much more.

Depending on your interest, once you set up your page and get your information collected, you can immediately start joining groups. For example, if you want to join some gold prospecting groups in your particular state, just type "<state> gold" in the search bar. Before you can click on the magnifying glass that serves as the search icon, you'll start to see options.

It's easy from there to start joining up and quickly expanding your social network. You can start learning about groups' calendars, upcoming events, issues, etc. You can "friend" the folks you meet and start following their posts and conversations; you can post your own questions as well.

As another example, if you live in Nebraska and want to find rocks and minerals, you can try searching on "Nebraska Rocks and Minerals." This search should turn up a link to the Hastings Museum in Nebraska. After you browse through their pages and check out their rocks, minerals, and fossils, return to their home page. Notice the row of buttons up in the left corner after "Follow us" where you can connect via Facebook. Click on the "f" button or a "Like" button and become a fan, send a message, check their information, and more. You will also start to notice targeted advertisements along the right column for services and products that might actually be of interest.

Not all groups are active, but you can usually prime the pump by posting an interesting picture or a provocative question. Asking for help as a newcomer, or "newbie," is perfectly acceptable in these groups.

Here is another way to charge up your Facebook page. If you browse over to www.sciencedaily.com and find something interesting, you can "like" it on your Facebook page and post a link with a comment and a picture. The site has continual updates about fossils, lost civilizations, geology, and volcanoes, to name a few topics. By clicking on the magic "f" button under these pages, you can post a link to the story right on your site. The link usually comes with a thumbnail picture that identifies it. That makes it easy to share cool stories rather than having to type individual e-mails or copy URLs for all your friends.

YouTube

www.youtube.com

No discussion of modern rockhounding and prospecting would be complete without directing you to YouTube. Anyone can now put together a simple video of his or her latest trip or accomplishment, and there are thousands of hours of entertainment now available. For example, check out this "World of Geology" grouping found at www.youtube.com/watch?v=RvIb85fyPiw. The number of people who have contributed small vignettes and stories about gold prospecting and mineral collecting continues to grow. In general these videos are very helpful—they show techniques and materials to beginners, as well as advertise easy places to collect.

There are videos on just about everything connected to collecting geological specimens, including:

Agate picking	Knapping
Collecting quartz crystals	Metal detecting
Diamond recovery	Meteorite hunting
Gold panning	Separating gold from black
Gold dredging and high-	sands
banking	Sluicing
Jade hunting	Wire-wrapping and lapidary

Whenever you start planning a trip to a new area, you might find a helpful video that shows what the area actually looks like. For example, if you organize an expedition to Bodie, California, there are already dozens of videos posted that show old black-and-white photos as well as modern views of the area. You can get a good sense for how hot, dry, and desolate the Bodie area really is.

Depending on your goal, you can either spread the word about interesting locales, products, or techniques or can angle for your own reality TV show. If you always approach your work with the idea of sharing, you will never disappoint.

YouTube has a feature that allows you to subscribe to someone's work so that you get a message when he or she posts a new video. Most of the videos are "one-hit wonders," but some enthusiasts seriously want to boost their number of subscribers, so help them out if you can.

Blogging

Blogs are another great vehicle for sharing information about field locales, collecting techniques, and success stories. Many times when you enter a search string into your web browser, you end up investigating personal web logs (blogs) that celebrate a contributor's many journeys. The information can be spot-on fascinating if it pertains to an area you are thinking of exploring.

Here is an example. ReBecca Hunt-Foster is a longtime paleontologist in the United States who writes a blog titled *Paleochick*. The website is http://paleochick.tumblr.com. She contributes "random postings on Geology and Paleontology with a bit of spunk and sass thrown in." For anyone remotely interested in fossils, it is a great read. She has written

Volcanic Blogger

Dave Tucker is a volcano geologist and geology educator at Western Washington University and is currently one of the directors of the Mount Baker Volcano Research Center (MBVRC) in Northwest Washington. His blog is at http://nwgeology.wordpress .com.

I do something geologic virtually every day. I write up field trips to post on my blog, *Northwest Geology Field Trips,* and occasional articles and updates for the MBVRC blog and website. Some days I teach geology to a group of homeschooled middle-school kids. Or I assist geology grad students at WWU who are focusing on aspects of Mount Baker geology. I am also writing a "people's geology guide," *Geology Underfoot in Western Washington.*

When I'm not in the field or in front of a classroom, I can spend hours and hours on my computer. I e-mail geologists all over the world daily and maintain two blogs. You can't be afraid of writing, and you have to be able to communicate well. The geo-blogosphere is huge—the public's thirst for geology education continues to grow.

about museum projects, job postings for field paleontologists, and even the celebration of the 374th birthday of Nicolas Steno.

Buried in her many years of posts are some very interesting and detailed descriptions of trilobite digs. She is diligent about publishing write-ups from her fieldwork, and even tosses in some video from time to time. Her blog is an excellent example of the real spirit of the Internet, which is to provide a cheap, easy method for contributing and locating information among like-minded individuals.

Here is another, more geological blog: www.nwgeology.wordpress .com. Dave Tucker is a research associate at Western Washington University in Bellingham, Washington, and he is a publishing whirlwind. He conducts guided geology field trips to western Washington geology locales, teaches geology at WWU, and is writing a book about Washington geology. In between all that, he manages to post frequently about glacial erratics, enormous landslides, fossil bird tracks, and more.

One resource that Hunt-Foster and Tucker both share is a link to more blogs from their respective pages. Tucker also links to the "granddaddy" of all geological blogs: *Geobulletin,* at www.geobulletin.org.

It is beyond the scope of this book to list all pertinent blogs, but the chief takeaway is this: Blogs can be a worthwhile source of information. You never know what you might find. Consider starting your own so that you can give back to the community.

In case you are wondering, the author maintains an infrequent blog at http://writingdocs.blogspot.com.

Twitter

http://twitter.com

Since Tweets are restricted to 140 characters or less, Twitter does not lend itself to Internet research. What Twitter can do is get the word out and advertise events such as field trips, museum exhibits, lectures, and book-signings. Or, if you find a provocative article or blog posting, you can Tweet that out to your like-minded friends.

LinkedIn

www.linkedin.com

Facebook is great for social stuff, updating your status, and uploading fun photos, but use LinkedIn for the professional side of life. It's like a permanent web presence for your résumé. If you put some effort into it, continually collect business cards, and reach out to folks who share your interests, you can build up your list of professional rockhounding and prospecting contacts. Once you do, you will be well on the way to making the transition from prospector to professional miner.

For example, when you go to a rock and gem show or a mining jubilee, take some time to collect business cards there. Put a notation on the back so you know the date of the show, and list anything you talked about with that person or any interesting equipment he or she built or represented. Once you get back home, pile up your business cards and search each person out on LinkedIn.

Mailing Lists

One early method for sharing information among enthusiasts still lives—the e-mail mailing list. Basically, users subscribe to a list and receive "posts." Instead of sending an e-mail to a few friends, you send it out to everyone subscribed to the list. You can get debates, arguments, advice, current events, and other information. Sometimes the activity is heavy; sometimes it quiets down.

Rockhounds have long relied on the Rock Net e-mail list, founded by Bob's Rock Shop and located at www.rockhounds.com/rocknet.

Fossil hunters can use Paleolist; instructions for joining are available at http://two.pairlist.net/mailman/listinfo/paleolist.

Gold prospectors seem to hang out more on forums, but check www.goldprospecting.com to join their e-mail list.

Meteorite hunters can go to http://six.pairlist.net/mailman/listinfo/meteorite-list to sign up for an active, passionate e-mail list all about meteorites.

There are other e-mail lists for lapidary, faceting, casting, and more. Check this link to find out more: www.rockhounds.com/rockshop/llist5.shtml.

HISTORICAL WEBSITES

The following list is by no means exhaustive; sites come and go quickly, and you'll want to learn to follow links and resources on your own, hang out at bulletin boards, etc. But it's a good start.

Mines and Mills

The USGS website is a prime resource for rockhounds, gold prospectors, and fossil hunters. We've already talked about the USGS in terms of educational material for basic geology, but the site is rich in resources beyond that. As just one example, check out the Mines and Mills map page at http://minerals.usgs.gov/minerals/pubs/mapdata. You can truly put your mapping skills to work here.

Western Mining History

www.westernmininghistory.com/minesmap

The old saying "Gold is where you find it" is true. However, if you believe those old prospectors knew what they were doing, you have to admit that nowadays, "Gold is where *they* found it." By studying Western mining history, you can gain insight into the location of tailings piles and surrounding outcrops from old districts that are still likely to contain interesting mineralization; rockhounds and prospectors are often at home in the same locales.

After the fever of the first gold rush subsided, experienced prospectors spread out from California and sampled every major and minor river system in western North America. They were patient, and they were good. Therefore, it isn't too likely you are going to find gold in a general area that has not already been identified.

GhostTowns.com

Now it's time to think outside the box. One handy tool is Ghost Towns, at www.ghosttowns.com. The site covers Canada and all fifty US states with an interactive map and includes updated, crowd-sourced information, photos, and driving directions. For example, if you are interested in the remote Gold Hill area of Utah, there is an entry for Gold Hill. In a report posted in June 2000, a writer said a few residents still live there at various times of the year, adding, "The local mines are trying to reopen. This area is scattered with old mines and buildings if you take the time to find them." You can also find six pictures, including a nice landscape shot of the townsite and surrounding mountains. So now you know that you have to bring in all your water, stock up on supplies, and have a full tank of gas in a well-maintained four-wheel-drive vehicle if your expedition is going to succeed.

One problem with this site is an avalanche of ads in the form of animated gifs, including an annoying flashing ad for dedicated servers.

State Historical Societies

As you research mining districts for clues about significant mineral deposits, you can benefit from checking your state historical society. More and more online information is available at these sites. You can learn about the lives of miners and their dependents and otherwise fill in some of the backstory on places you intend to visit.

ONLINE MAPS

In this section we will look at some of the major mapping programs and websites you can use in planning your next assault. Using the old ghost town of Garnet, Montana, as a guide, you'll learn how you can view road maps, topographical maps, and high-resolution aerial photographs for anywhere in the Unite States. Between mapping software, satellite imagery, and GPS, there has never been a time when you could pull together so much information so easily.

There are several online map services available, including www. MapQuest.com, www. Maps.com, www. TargetMap.com, www. MyTopo .com, www. NationalGeographic.com, www. TerraServer.com, www. Click2Map.com, www. ZeeMaps.com, www. ESRI.com, www. Apple.com, www. Bing.com, and www. Maps4PC.com. Google Maps is free and easy, so we'll use it for demonstration purposes.

Google Maps

Over the last few years, there's been a tremendous investment of time and energy in Google Maps (www.maps.google.com), and being part of the open-source community means there are far more applications available that highlight locales and overlay information. Since Google Maps is like a web-based extension of Google Earth, we'll talk more about some of the best features a little later.

For illustration, on the next page is the Google Maps opening view for Garnet, Montana:

The terrain looks empty at this view, as there are no subtle topographic or geomorphologic features. The road names and numbers display; and key geographical features like mountains appear, but the map is relatively barren. That's because it is meant to be only a base; if you want to see terrain, you can flip the view and see a detailed terrain view. It's nice to be able to get a better idea of the topography and water features, for example. Or you can flip to the satellite imagery for a third view of an area.

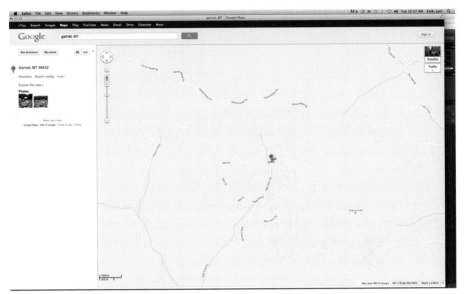

Google Maps general view for Garnet, Montana

Google Earth

What is Google Earth? Here is the corporate answer from early on:

> Google Earth is a computer system that interactively streams
> more than 10,000 gigabytes of Earth information (images,
> elevation, business data . . .) to personal computers over the
> Internet. As a Google Earth user you can explore the earth and
> zoom down to cities and points of interest, seeing buildings,
> roads, cars, and even people.

Not many of us have a hard drive that can store 10,000 gigabytes,
so to run Google Earth you need Internet access. Google Earth was
first developed by Keyhole, which was bought by Google in 2004. Go to
http://earth.google.com and find the link to download, or "Get Google
Earth (Free Version)." There are premium versions, but let's stick with
the basics for now. The download takes awhile—be patient. Follow the
prompts to run the setup and get started. The opening graphic is a big
round map of Earth featuring the United States.

Note the layers menu down on the lower left. Click to open up the
"More" listings, and experiment with what appeals to you. For example, one section reveals volcanoes, which might be of interest if you

are looking for obsidian. Since you will most likely be on public land for many of your travels, you'll probably want to reveal campgrounds, rest areas, picnic areas, and ranger offices under "More > Parks/Recreation Areas > USDA Forest Service." Both rockhounds and prospectors are often in search of water access to check gravel bars, so you should check the US Fish and Wildlife box. Under "More > Place Categories," you will probably want to include gas stations and grocery stores so that you know where you can fill up your vehicle and restock your ice chest.

Tailor Google Earth to your needs, and feel free to experiment to determine what information you need and what you don't. Every time you upgrade to a new version, be sure to poke around to see what's new.

Some remote areas still do not have the fullest resolution available, but you get enough of a picture to appreciate what is there. In more populated areas, such as where you live, you might be able to spot your rooftop. When at highest resolution, you can see cars on the street. The age of the photos varies, as does the season they were snapped, but most are taken in summer and are updated frequently. You can check the date of the photograph at the bottom of the image in the middle; to the lower left, you can see if older photos exist. If you click that icon, a slider displays on the top left, and you can see how conditions have changed over time.

Over on the left side of the bottom of the image, you can see the "Pointer" statistics. The latitude is carried out to six decimals, as is the longitude. Some of you may not be familiar with seeing latitude and longitude in a decimal format, but it can save you a lot of time. Trying to mess with degrees, minutes, and seconds can be frustrating. The bad news is that many USDA Forest Service maps are primarily in the old minutes and seconds format, so you may have to convert back and forth. To do this, click on "Tools" at the top of Google Earth and select "Options" at the bottom of the Tools menu. Under the 3D View tab, you can see the different GPS format options available.

Decimal degree notation is the easiest to work with because you don't have to include so much extra data—or even symbols other than the negative sign. For Crater of Diamonds State Park, the GPS coordinates in decimal notation are simply 34.032600°, -93.671811°. Note that you can drop the degree symbols when you paste those numbers into Google Earth. That is much easier to use than 34° 1' 57.36" N, 93° 40' 18.52" W. It is also easier to cut and paste into other programs, such as

GeoCommunicator, or to build yourself a list of the key turns and landmarks you want to visit on your expedition.

Along the top of the screen, you will see a little yellow pushpin icon that you can use to put in your own place marks. When you click the icon, an untitled pushpin displays in the center of your view, as shown in the photo. You can title the place mark, cut and paste the latitude and longitude into the description, and leave yourself a note for later. Now when you click on the place mark, you will see the information you entered into that description box.

You can right-click on your place mark and get directions to or from the park. Enter in the city and state you are traveling from, and you can get an idea of the time and distance involved to travel to the diamond digs. A bold purple line should display on the Google Earth map, with key turns marked in. The route information also displays on the left, and you can see how many miles total the drive would be, plus mileage between key turns. You can "play" that route like a movie by clicking the "Play Tour" button, or get rid of that route by clicking the "X." Those road directions are usually good, but for real back roads, you should *always* verify them with a road atlas or purchase the relevant USDA Forest Service/Bureau of Land Management (BLM) map.

Before you exit the program, save your work. Go up to the File menu and click "Save," then "Save My Places" so that the marker stays put for the next time you use the program.

One weakness of Google Earth is naming creeks and rivers. The Terrain feature in Google Maps actually does a better job with those small gulches and streams that are crucial to older directions. Even Google Maps can let you down, however; you may have to rely on the detail available in the topo maps view of www.GeoCommunicator.gov, for example. (More on that later in this chapter.)

Another excellent tool here is the ruler, located up at the top of the page in the Tools menu. Click the ruler icon and click somewhere in the map, then click at a second point to get the distance between the two points. If you need to plot out the distance on an old road, switch to the Path feature. The running total distance displays as you keep clicking.

One last feature to explain is the compass. In the far upper right there is a faint compass overlaying the map. Use this to orient the map and square up north–south. You can also adjust the orientation to the horizon or the zoom if you do not have a wheel mouse.

Google Earth Community

You might be interested in some of the published methods used to fine-tune Google Earth. These are tried-and-true tricks for getting the most out of your system, as posted at the Google Earth Community website:

- **Adjust the cache.** Click the "Tools > Options > Cache" tab and set your disk cache as high as the maximum listed on the page. Set the memory cache to about half of your system RAM. The disk cache remembers your previous usage, so if you tend to go back to certain places, you'll go back faster than if you were doing it the first time. The memory cache holds the information from just seconds ago, which helps if you are trying to find something and keep going over an area. You should not have to tinker with these numbers once you set them.
- **Adjust the Detail Area.** From the "Tools > Options > 3D View" tab, check your Detail Area setting. A small Detail Area will be blurry at the edges but will download faster. If you do not like the blur, adjust to the way you want it.
- **Adjust the texture colors.** Also from the "Tools > Options > 3D View" tab, check the texture colors. There is a 16-bit and a 32-bit mode. Naturally, 32-bit is better. However, old notebooks, systems that do not have a separate video card, or systems with old video cards will want that 16-bit mode.

If these tricks do not help much, you may need a newer PC.

Advanced Users

Once you start to learn Google Earth, your next step is to join the Google Earth Community. This is real "Web 2.0" stuff, with users in control of the content. You will have to join Google Forums to do so, but it is an easy setup. Go to https://productforums.google.com/forum to get started.

You might notice that scattered throughout Google Earth there are embedded photographs uploaded by users, marked as light-blue "Panaramio" boxes in the landscape. These are the same photos that display in Google Maps, as shown for Garnet, Montana. If you want to learn how to upload your own landscape photos, point your browser to www.panoramio.com and set up an account. Then check out the various groups. You will probably like the Nature and Geography section. There is a great group for pictures of gold dredges, for example.

Another hot spot for Google Earth information is back at the main Google Earth site. Go to http://earth.google.com/gallery/ and check out the user information there. Users have posted all kinds of information, including movies about rising sea level, the growth of the city of London, and various hurricanes.

Also check out the Google Earth blog at http://gearthblog.com. This is an unofficial site, but it's full of amazing information.

Google Earth can make you much more comfortable before you visit a spot for the first time. "Seeing" the area, even from aerial photography, really comes in handy. As more prospectors start to harness the Internet, we should be able to share our photographs and experiences and make even more content available.

Overlays

Being open-source at heart, Google Earth has seen some wonderful additions, or "hacks," by users all over the world. Here is one web page to start: www.gearthhacks.com. It is a wonder to behold, and worth dipping a toe into.

Overlay files are denoted by a ".kmz" file extension. Download the ".kmz" file, and save it to your desktop; then in Google Earth, go to "File > Open" and point to the file.

It is hard to know where to stop when using Google Earth for your research. Here is a page with all kinds of information and tools at Carleton College: http://serc.carleton.edu/NAGTWorkshops/visualize04/tool_examples/google_earth.html. You can find the tools you need to make your own overlays and much more.

Here is a set of Google Earth overlays with a physical science theme: http://classroom.sdmesa.net/dbarrie/google_earth_overlays.htm. There are tours of Devils Tower, Wyoming, various faults and volcanoes, and much more.

MineCache

www.minecache.com

This Google Earth overlay costs a little bit, but it has superb information for gold prospectors and mineral collectors. Use MineCache as an online gold mine mapping tool to help you narrow down your gold prospecting locations.

Meteorites

There are Google Earth tools for many different meteorite tasks. You can look for deserts, or maybe try to find a recent crater. In 2008 an Australian used Google Earth to locate a meteorite crater in Australia. Check it out at www.cosmosmagazine.com/news/1934/aussie-finds -meteorite-crater-google-earth.

In 2010 a researcher used Google Earth to discover meteorite craters in the Egyptian desert: http://wattsupwiththat.com/2010/09/24/ google-earth-leads-to-spectacular-meteor-crater-find.

For a Google Map overlay of US meteorite finds, go to http://meteorite .weebly.com/meteorite-falls-map.html.

One exciting spot to check out is the Earth Impact Database at www .passc.net/EarthImpactDatabase/index.html. You will see all the various known impact sites mapped on Earth.

Here is a link to 26,000 worldwide meteorite impacts in a Google Earth overlay: https://productforums.google.com/forum/?fromgroups= #!topic/gec-places/59UqlWKj9Gg[1-25].

Here's another meteorite impact sites overlay, created by Michael Gill: www.freelists.org/post/az-observing/Meteorite-Impact -Site-Overlay-for-Google-Earth.

And finally, if you want to join in the search for large space rocks, a user recently found a large asteroid using Google Sky. You can find the YouTube video with an easy search. The Meteorites USA page has good videos at www.meteoritesusa.com/meteorite-videos.htm.

Free Tools

You can learn to make your own topographic map overlays for Google Earth at Free Geography Tools: http://freegeographytools.com/2009/ usgs-topographic-map-overlays-for-google-earth.

Mineral Resources Data System (MRDS)

This USGS database lists information on more than 300,000 sites in the United States at http://tin.er.usgs.gov/mrds/help.html.

The system has two primary functions:

1. **Research and assessment.** Provides information for land planners and decision makers about where mineral commodities are known and suspected in Earth's crust and about the environmental

consequences of the presence of those commodities. MRP supports an ongoing effort to coordinate the development of national-scale geologic, geochemical, geophysical, and mineral resource databases and the migration of existing databases to standard models and formats that are available to both internal and external users.

2. **Data collection, analysis, and dissemination.** Describes current production and consumption of about one hundred mineral commodities, both domestically and internationally, for approximately 180 countries.

A tutorial for the database is available at www.mindat.org/article .php/485/Google+Earth+Meets+MRDS%3A+A+Basic+Tutorial.

GeoCommunicator

Topographic maps are excellent resources for identifying mines, pits, tailings, gravel bars, and other features of interest to field collectors. There was a time when it took months to identify which topo map you needed and then order it from a warehouse in Denver and wait for the big cardboard tube to arrive. Later, a site called www.Topozone.com was an excellent resource for online topographical maps, but it was purchased by www.Trails.com and is no longer free. Fortunately the USGS put out the interactive map sets at www.geocommunicator.gov.

The main interactive maps page at www.GeoCommunicator.gov provides access to topo maps for all fifty states.

By clicking and zooming and grabbing, you can orient the map down to a specific site you want to see in detail.

Here are some of the symbols that are particularly interesting:

Table 2: Topo Map Symbols of Special Interest to Collectors and Prospectors

Icon	Description
Gravel Pit	Gravel pits can be either round river rock, ideal for agate picking, or angular chunks of basalt used for gravel roads. Look for quartz and agate seams and vugs of zeolite crystals in basalt quarries.
Borrow Pit	Borrow pits are usually places to gather fill material, especially soil. These sites typically are not of interest to rockhounds and prospectors.
	Simple designations of "pit" can mean a gravel pit or a borrow pit. The brown stipple pattern can indicate large areas of disturbed earth.
	Gravels are marked by larger stippling along beaches and moving water. The word *gravel* sometimes accompanies these markings, but usually gravel exposures are so large that the mapmakers leave out the text. These areas can be ideal for rockhounding, especially when the gravels are sorted and clean.
Tailings	Tailings piles can stretch for hundreds of square acres and are usually only of interest because they indicate a large dredging or mining operation was nearby. Some dredge fields are worth inspecting with a metal detector for big nuggets or simply to look for interesting rocks discarded by the miners.

Icon	Description
Prospects	Prospects are marked by a simple "X" and usually indicate some kind of disturbed earth. In many cases, the disturbance can be quite minor, such as barely a few shovels of dirt moved. Prospects are *not* mines. Still, they show where someone invested some labor for something.
	Adits are the typical tunnels associated with mining. The symbol is a *Y* that is oriented the way the tunnel appears on the ground. Adits are obviously dangerous and are not a place for small children or pets. Again, they are good signs that there was something worth working for here.
Mapleton Mine	A box that is half filled in on the diagonal denotes fully developed mines with a vertical shaft for hoisting ore to the surface. These are obviously just as dangerous as adits, if not more so, as they go straight down. They indicate a significant investment in extracting geological treasures, so they are worth finding on the map.
	Placer mines are not always marked with "placer" text, and they use the same hammer-and-pick icon as quarries use. Older placer mines are often hard to detect unless there are still tailings around. Flooding tends to wash away most signs of placer activity.
Quarry	Quarries are obviously of interest to rockhounds, as they usually have large cliff faces to inspect for veins, vugs, and mineral showings. Many quarries exploit interesting rocks hard enough to take a polish, such as marble and granite. Flooding can make these dangerous places; most good quarries for rockhounding are on private land, and permission is required to enter.
Quarry	Quarries designated with the "pit" stippling rather than the hammer and pick are usually big open pit areas that caved in or were reclaimed. In limestone areas, these are of interest to fossil hunters.

There are settings at the bottom right corner of the display for an aerial photo view, a topo map, roads only, and the almost-empty base map. Since it takes a few seconds to redraw the map when the system is slow, you can use the base map setting to move around quickly, and

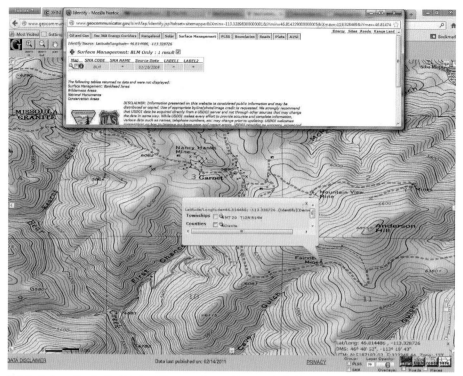

Detailed information for the Fairview Mine, near Garnet, Montana, including GPS coordinates

then switch to more detailed views when you are getting close to where you want to explore.

Up along the top, there is a ribbon of icons for various features. If you click on the Identify icon, you could put the cursor directly on the adit symbol for the Fairview Mine and get even more information.

Before February 2011 you could also pull up specific mining claim information, and you could overlay the current and expired claim boundaries. This was a great tool for checking to see if there was current, active interest in a mining district, and you could see if there were any expired claims that you might want to explore further. Alas, this feature went away due to budget cuts.

Note that you can "publish" or print your view by clicking the Adobe PDF button, which makes it easy to create screen shots. You can also cut and paste various GPS coordinates and arm yourself with an entire checklist if you want to inspect several adits, mine shafts, and prospects for an area. You may not need coordinates for each prospect, but if you at least bring the coordinates for named features, you can quickly orient yourself when in the field.

Gigapan

Creating your own large-scale photographic panoramas is getting easier with the new software in modern cameras. Check out www.gigapan.org to see how these images have such a massive scale that geologists can use them and share the information.

ARCGIS

ArcGIS Explorer allows people to share maps, data, and tools online. There is also a desktop version available for those who do not have high-speed access.

Here is the site: http://explorer.arcgis.com. You need to have Microsoft Silverlight installed, which can be daunting, and will likely change. The page loads slowly, but eventually you should bring up the featured content.

Since there is no telling what the site managers might choose to highlight from day to day, you will want to learn to search the contents to find what you are looking for. Type "geology" into the Find Maps & Groups box and press the Enter button. You should get a few pages of geology-themed maps to check out.

There are topographic maps, hazard maps, and maps showing mine dangers, earthquake locations, and lots more. Check the Community Geology Base map, which covers North America. You can zoom in to your state and watch as it dynamically loads the data at different scales. Most of us have a scroll mouse now, and this will zoom in and zoom out on the data.

ArcGIS is great for building geology maps. For example, if you are gearing up for a visit to the Burnt River area of eastern Oregon, you can pull data to help figure out the relationships between rock units you will encounter in the field. The geology here is old and complicated, with Jurassic and Cretaceous granite intrusions colored pink and labeled *JKg*, recent Quaternary river gravels and alluvium colored yellow and labeled *Qal*, and so forth. You can see the geological map in the screen shot.

One feature that will help you with the geology is the Identify button up in the ribbon at the top of the page. The most common reason to do this would be to learn more about a particular color on the map,

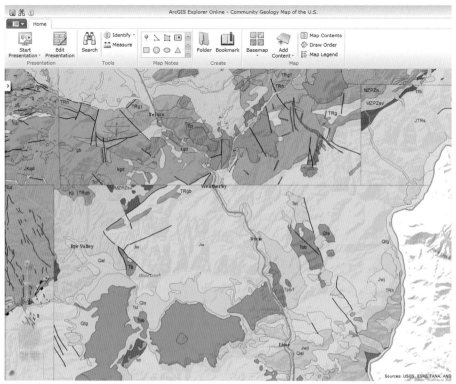

ArcGIS geology map for the Burnt River, Oregon, vicinity

which represents a rock type, formation, or other major unit. Click this button and you should be able to then left-click inside the map for more information.

Sometimes you will get a formation name, age, and rock type. Other times you won't get much more than the age of the rock. There are often links to the source map, so you can chase down detailed geology from there.

You can use a topographic map as the base, using the Basemap icon in the ribbon. You can go with various satellite images as well.

ArcGIS Explorer allows people who do not have a GIS or a mapping background to create and easily make, use, or view maps. You could add you own data to existing maps to create your own custom maps. You can even code your own maps that are shared on that site and combine data from multiple other maps or servers. You could plug in your GPS, use the data in GIS or other programs, and add it to the web maps. In short, there is a lot of power here.

Modern-day prospectors have great tools at their disposal, so it is a shame not to use them.

GEOLOGY MAPS

If there is one item every field collector knows how to use, it is a map. We surround ourselves with maps—highway maps, forest service maps, topographic maps, and even screen captures of Google Maps. Yet many budding prospectors leave out one of the most important maps of all: the geology map. They worry that the terms and concepts will be overwhelming, but you can improve your odds.

Perhaps you have seen a geology map in the past. They are usually set on a base map and then splashed with vivid colors. But you may not know how to read them, or you may not understand how much better your prospecting can be with a relevant geology map in your possession. In this section, we will take a beginner's look at several different kinds of geology maps and show you how to use that information to gain more success on your next trip into the field.

State Geology Maps

First let's look at an old postcard-size geology map of Montana, shown on the next page. You can see one thing right away: The eastern part of the state is fairly "boring." Two colors mark the majority of the geology from Billings east: Cenozoic deposits and Mesozoic deposits. But what does that mean?

Geologic time periods take some memorizing, and they are not regular in intervals or coverage. First off, there are two eons. Earliest is the Precambrian, which is all the time when there was no life on Earth. Second is all the time there *has* been life on the planet. This eon is called the Phanerozoic, which started about 544 million years ago with the dawn of the Cambrian period.

To get started, look at the old rocks first. The Precambrian includes the Proterozoic, Archeozoic, and Hadean eras. These rocks have usually been cooked, heated, pressurized, folded, and intensely metamorphosed. They are known as the "Superbelt" series in northern Idaho and northwestern Montana and are the source of the incredible silver deposits near Wallace, Idaho. You just have to remember that the Precambrian eon stretches from the birth of our planet, about 4.6 billion years ago, to the

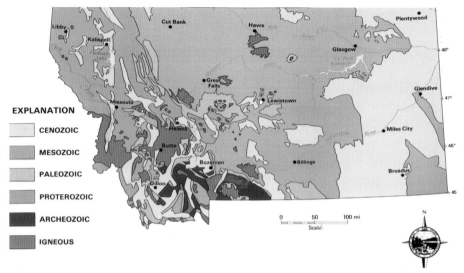

EXPLANATION

- CENOZOIC
- MESOZOIC
- PALEOZOIC
- PROTEROZOIC
- ARCHEOZOIC
- IGNEOUS

Generalized geology map for the state of Montana

explosion of life much later, about 544 million years ago. The Cambrian is marked by the first evidence of something beyond blue-green algae.

The Phanerozoic era is broken down further into three eras: the Paleozoic, Mesozoic, and Cenozoic. Start with the oldest, the Paleozoic: This is the time when trilobites evolved into reptiles. To help keep it straight, remember that the Mesozoic era was so-named because *meso* means "middle." This is the period of about 180 million years in duration that we associate with dinosaurs—the Triassic, Jurassic, and Cretaceous periods. After that, the younger rocks are gathered into the Cenozoic, the one still growing, and stretch from about sixty-five million years ago to present day.

Clearly, if you were looking for dinosaur fossils, eastern Montana's Mesozoic rocks would be the place to start. Judging from the jumble of old rocks and igneous masses in western Montana, gold prospectors would want to look around Helena, Butte, and Dillon. Prospectors know that when big granite intrusions poke their way through the upper crust, the outside margins are likely spots to search for all kinds of interesting mineral specimens in the quartz veins. Given that knowledge, it would make sense in a general way to look for evidence of gold claims around Helena, where igneous rocks are in contact with older Paleozoic rocks.

That is the key to understanding geology maps. They show what rocks to expect on the surface if you are in that area. Geology maps also show a three-dimensional view of what lies beneath the surface. More on that later.

Online Geology Maps
In addition to the tons of updated geological information at About.com Geology, there is a link to state geologic and physiographic maps:

http://geology.about.com/od/stategeologicmaps/Geologic_Maps_of_the_US_States.htm.

The site also has helpful links to state geological departments, such as www.iowagold.com/LINKSPAGES/gold_links_usgs.htm, where you can often find old geology reports for mining districts.

Stratigraphy and Nicholas Steno
Notice that the explanation scale on the bottom left of the Montana geology map is ranked from youngest (on top) to oldest (on the bottom). The scale thus mimics what you would expect to find in the field—the oldest rocks are at the bottom of the cliff. This holds true about 99.9 percent of the time and is known as the concept of "superposition."

The concept of young rocks sitting on top of old rocks is credited to Nicholas Steno (1638–86), a genius with a scalpel who discovered the saliva gland and tear gland during his medical career. He was an equally keen observer of the physical world and grappled with a curiosity of the time: how fossil clams and snails came to rest at the top of certain mountains in Europe. In the 2003 book, *The Seashell on the Mountaintop: A Story of Science Sainthood and the Humble Genius Who Discovered a New History of the Earth,* author Alan Cutler described the life of Steno. The young scholar was concerned that religion and science must somehow coexist and believed that many church teachings were seriously flawed because they utterly ignored scientific principles. He hoped that religion could be reconciled with observable facts, rather than always being at odds with rigorous fieldwork.

Steno's contemporaries believed fossils somehow "spawned" in rocks over time, or perhaps even fell like rain from the heavens at night. Steno watched spring floods washing down torrents full of sediments mixed with organic matter and noted the repeated processes of a young and restless Earth. He published his findings in *De Solido,* explaining that Earth is far older than previously thought. He described how layer after layer of rock is put down, how time can harden these sediments, and how fossil-bearing strata can end up at the very top of a mountain peak.

But his religious beliefs were strong as well. Following the publication of his findings, Steno converted to Catholicism, retreated into an ascetic lifestyle, and became a missionary. He earned the rank of bishop and then died fairly young and in poverty. In 1988 Steno was named a saint.

Old Mining District Maps

Gold prospectors appreciate Steno's observations, because we also see streams and rivers moving sediments around constantly. It is that movement of material in a flood-stage creek that refreshes gravel bars each spring. So now consider a second geology map at this point—the old-fashioned black-and-white district map.

The image shown is a simple geologic map from J. S. Diller's study, *The Auriferous Gravels of the Trinity River Basin, California.* In this drawing, Diller was trying only to show the relationship between older and younger gravels near Douglas City, south of Weaverville. As anyone who has been to the GPAA claim at Douglas City knows, there are numerous tailings piles in this area. Tons of gravels have been washed and

Detailed, hand-drawn map of the Douglas City, California, gold fields

piled along the Trinity River here. Miners quickly noted that some gravels were laid down so long ago that they had been hardened. Diller wrote that these "gravels of the second cycle" were cemented together, and thus it was very difficult to set up a big hydraulic operation to work them. Water at very high pressure was unable to blast these gravels apart.

Not so the most recent sedimentary structures, he reported:

> The gravels of the third cycle are confined to the canyons and narrow valleys of the present streams and include not only the gravels capping the terraces on the valley slopes but also those in the present stream beds. . . . In general, the gravels of the

third cycle should contain the most highly concentrated values. Furthermore, they can be most easily and economically mined, because they are entirely un-cemented and most readily reached by water for piping. These are the gravels so extensively mined in the early days. . . . The most available and probably the richest have been washed away, but still there is much left that may pay well for economical mining on a large scale." (p. 26)

Armed with this type of detailed information, you're better able to figure out which gravels you are in once you reach Douglas City. Right along the road near the old GPAA claim, you will find an adit driven straight in on a contact with bedrock and the gravels of the second cycle. Interestingly, there were decent-size platinum nuggets in this cemented gravel.

Modern Geology Map

Next we will look at a modern geology map from the Granite Creek district of northern Oregon.

The map shows the placer diggings along Granite Creek, about 5 miles northwest from the town of Granite. Remember from the Montana

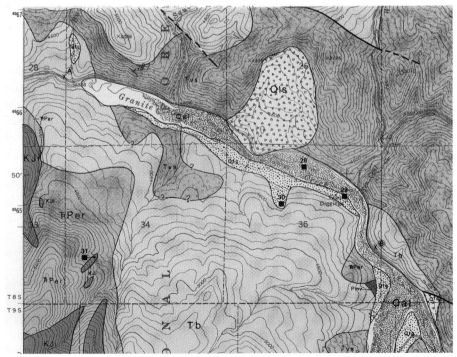

Excerpt from a geology map for Granite Creek, Oregon, showing dredged areas and old placer claims

map that the Cenozoic rocks were marked in yellow? In fact, the Cenozoic is split into seven epochs: Paleocene, Eocene, Oligocene, Miocene, Pliocene, Pleistocene, and last, or youngest, the Holocene. Now it gets tricky. At one point geologic eras were marked as the first, second, third, and fourth—or primary, secondary, tertiary, and quaternary. The Holocene is equivalent to the Quaternary and began somewhere between 1.8 million and 2.6 million years ago. Most of the soil, sand, and gravel along creeks and rivers are marked on a geology map as some kind of Quaternary deposit—usually alluvium (a fancy word for water-deposited sediment).

Map Explanation

Notice that there are at least three different types of yellow markings that describe the deposits along Granite Creek. Those are defined in the following "explanation column," which is a key part of a geology map.

The geologists who mapped the Granite Creek area identified four different Quaternary deposits:

QAL stands for Quaternary alluvium and is found on almost every geology map published. The color is usually just plain yellow, with no other notations. For a gold miner, the chance to work some "gravel, sand, and silt in channels and flood plains" sounds good.

QLS, or Quaternary landslide debris, does not sound nearly as profitable. The map usually shows a yellow coloration, with tiny blue triangles at random angles. Unless the landslide came right off a contact between granite and older rock, it would not be worthwhile to work for gold.

QGM, or Quaternary glacial moraine, is equally suspect for gold prospecting. The map usually shows yellow coloration with small blue dots of random size. Because they scraped the bedrock clean, glaciers rarely concentrated heavy gold values.

QTG, or Quaternary terrace gravels, are a gold prospector's friend. The map usually shows yellow coloration with tiny black dots. The terrace deposits around Granite Creek are "poorly sorted fluviatile deposits of gravel, sand, and silt situated at higher levels than the flood plains of present streams." That's good—that's like finding an old stream or riverbed (the Latin word for river is *fluvius.*) The only thing missing from the description is the word *auriferous,* from the Latin word for gold, *aurum.*

On some maps of heavily dredged areas, you will see a *Qt* for tailings, but most of the time they are just marked as "tailings" in the usual yellow Quaternary deposits.

Stratigraphic Column

Geologists like to further define the time relationship between deposits with the concept of a stratigraphic column, here labeled as a "Time Rock Chart." This graphic shows the ages for each stratum, or distinct rock layer, as the strata would be found in a cliff or outcrop. Again, the youngest rocks are at the top. At Granite Creek, the common alluvium is the youngest deposit and the terrace gravels are oldest, but they may overlap with glacial moraine in places.

You can also see that there was a lot of activity in this area during the Eocene and Oligocene. This was the period in Oregon marked by extensive basalt flows and accompanying ash deposits.

In particular, note the presence of *Tgt*—tertiary gravel terraces. In the explanation, the geologists report the following: "Locally, the deposits have been mined for placer gold, especially where the gravels have been reworked by modern streams." Bingo!

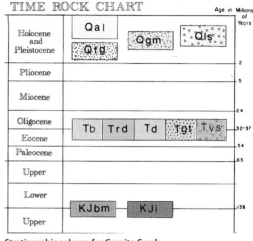

Stratigraphic column for Granite Creek

Also note the red boxes at the bottom, marked *KJbm* and *KJi*. The letter *K* is the geologic symbol for the Cretaceous, the last period in the Mesozoic, known as the Age of Reptiles. The letter *J* is the symbol for the Jurassic, even older, which we all recognize from the movie *Jurassic Park* and thus understand was also during the Age of Reptiles. The geologist chose the smaller letters *bm* to stand for the Blue Mountains, and the lower case *i* is a common symbol for granite intrusive. In this case, the granite, which has radioactive elements associated with its magnetite grains, has been dated to 135 million years old, near the boundary between the Cretaceous and the Jurassic.

Cross-sections

The next piece to look at on a geology map is the structure under the ground. This is where geology maps go from one dimension to two and, with a little imagination, to three dimensions. It's one thing to know what kind of rock you are walking on. It is quite another to understand what is going on far beneath the surface. Most geology maps include some kind of cross-section of the surface deposits, such as in the map shown here:

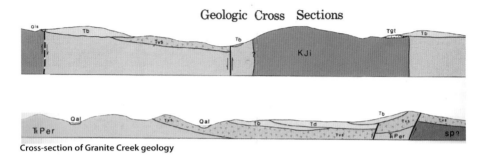

Geologic Cross Sections

Cross-section of Granite Creek geology

Here is where things get tricky. Sometimes rocks are stacked on top of other rocks in a nice, neat order, just like a layer cake. Other times the rocks are all jumbled up. Here at Granite Creek you can see a big red granite intrusive, *KJi,* flanked on both ends by light gray *TrPer,* a Triassic-Permian Elkhorn Ridge argillite. The question mark on the left edge means nobody is really sure of the exact location of the contact between the two rocks. In some spots there are bands of *Tvs,* then *Tb,* then *Tg.* You can also see the way Quaternary alluvium, *Qal,* sits in the little valleys in the Tertiary volcanics.

Things get even more complicated from here. There are symbols on the geology map that show strike and dip for the rocks, which is a way of defining how the rocks tilt and in what direction. We know most (but not all!) sedimentary rocks were originally deposited very close to horizontal. After they get shoved around by intrusions and faults, the beds tip. It takes a particular instrument, a Brunton compass, to get the strike and dip; most of you don't have one—so we can move on.

There are many different kinds of faults—known, mapped, inferred, and assumed. The more positive the geologist is, the more solid the fault line that is drawn on the map. Some faults are shown as dashed lines, meaning they are inferred or assumed. Other faults might have the direction of their movement recorded on the geology map. Again, these are sometimes important for prospectors, as some mines exploit quartz veins that intrude along faults.

Veins and Adits

Up to now, we have mostly talked about how placer miners can use geology maps. Let's turn now to hard rock mining.

The accompanying map shows some of hard rock mines east of Lightning Creek, near Granite, Oregon, with their accompanying vein systems. Veins that outcrop at the surface are marked in a thick or dotted red line, depending on whether they are actually mapped or just inferred. On this map, which shows an area west of Granite on the road to Greenhorn, you can see the big granite intrusive, with the many mines and prospects marked in black squares. Each of these mines is described elsewhere on the map, but that is not the norm on most geology maps.

There are other symbols on the map as well. As you can see, there are many old mines in this area, and you would expect to get some interesting samples from any tailings pile you could reach.

Better yet, try to find the Quebec or Alamo Mines and collect where the vein system crops out. Those should be especially rewarding, if they are not on private land. Note also that there appears to be two patches of *Tgt*—those gold-bearing terrace gravels—right along the jeep trail that leads to Buck Gulch. No wonder the Lightning Creek placers are located where they are. This is the primary place where you would hope there are no current claims or patented land, because if the land is open, it could contain unworked, original material.

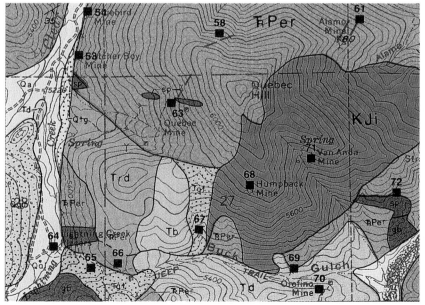

Vein system and mines around Lightning Creek

Final Thoughts on Geology Maps

Reading and understanding a geology map can be confusing at first, but a little experience should help make you a better prospector. You may not know what some of the fancy geology words mean when you get started, but you can find the definitions in this book, on the Internet, or from a good geology textbook. The key is to keep pushing yourself until you start to pick up the terms, almost like a language.

If you join a club where you can talk with other members on a regular basis, they can help you with your challenges, like pronouncing alluvium (uh-LOO-vee-um). Also, take comfort in the fact that this science is very young. There were no true geology maps until the early 1800s, when William Smith drew a complete geology map of England. His work is described by Simon Winchester in the excellent book *The Map That Changed the World*:

> [Smith] understood for the first time that geology was a science requiring observations in three dimensions. He could make maps and make surveys of the visible upper dimensions of the landscape with ease—anyone with a modicum of skill could do that. But to see *below* the surface, to observe or extrapolate the imaginable third dimension underground—that was a new skill, possessed by very few, and yet that had a potential that Smith was soon going to recognize and exploit."
> (p. 74)

Some states are starting to post geology maps on the web, usually as a PDF that maintains its precision as you zoom down. Other states still sell their maps, and they can be on the expensive side. Many universities maintain a collection of USGS reports, which are very helpful for those old hand-drawn, black-and-white maps. iGeology is an app for iPhones that lets you take a geological map of Britain with you and ties into the phone's GPS.

The next time you plan an expedition to a mining district, whether you are seeking gold or interesting minerals on the dumps, see if you can find any geology maps or write-ups for the locale. If such reports exist, you can greatly increase your odds by knowing the geology in advance.

JSTOR SEARCHES

www.jstor.org

JSTOR is a not-for-profit service that includes full-text content of more than 1,400 academic journals, as well as thousands of primary sources. There is a wealth of paleontological information available for fossil hunters, and there is plenty of geology to sift through. The service connects libraries, researchers, teachers, and students around the world with vital scholarly content in more than fifty disciplines. JSTOR recently added more than 15,000 scholarly books from a leading roster of academic presses and scholarly publishers. Your online research will be faster, easier, and more effective, but there is a fee. According to its website, the ultimate goal is to "make JSTOR available to everyone who wants access to it, while doing so in a way that ensures sustainability of the service."

JSTOR isn't the only service out there. A trained information professional and/or reference librarian can help you immensely as you try to track down academic information and research. Guy Kawasaki, famed Silicon Valley entrepreneur and early Apple Computer pioneer, had the following advice for anyone who wanted to get ahead in high-tech: "Suck up to a librarian." His advice applies to geological research as well.

BUILD YOUR OWN BOOK

One planning chore to master is making your own book of maps, write-ups, and other resources that you can bring to the field. You can use Microsoft Office tools such as PowerPoint to create a giant "presentation" for yourself so that you can save wear and tear on your nicest books or maps. The great thing about PowerPoint is that you can insert large photos, and when you run the presentation or print your copy, the map or photo fills the entire screen at a decent resolution. As a printout in landscape mode, you have plenty of real estate to zoom in or out, and you can annotate your maps with arrows, text boxes, call-outs, and even bleed tabs.

There are a couple of methods to capture images from the web. First you can try the old right-click move. Hold the mouse over the image and click the right-hand mouse button. You should get a menu with options to "Save Image As," which will let you download the picture to your desktop or your hard drive.

If you do not get that menu, there are two more options. One is to hit the Print Screen button on your keyboard. When you do, you save the entire screen image to your computer's "clipboard." You will then need a graphics program such as Adobe Photoshop, which lets you open the image, create a new file, and see the image after you "Edit > Paste." From here you can crop to what you want to keep and then save the image.

Some users have advanced programs that take screen shots for them. If you are still using Windows XP, for example, your best bet is something like Full Shot, which lets you outline the region of the screen you want to save. It is a great tool, and you can use it to grab just the part of the map you want and then blow it up for a detailed view. A limited demo is available at http://www.inbit.com.

Windows 7 shipped with a built-in snipping tool in the Accessories menu. It also cuts out a spot from your screen, and you can save the image as a JPEG, which can be handy. Be sure to use some kind of logical file-naming convention.

If you are a new wagon master, piloting your first large caravan of vehicles, you can even print out copies for each driver and include cell phone numbers, emergency info, etc. Planning any expedition is a challenge and a lot of responsibility. On the one hand, nobody should have to rockhound or prospect alone. Yet the more people you have to plan for, the more that can go wrong. There is nothing like being in the middle of nowhere, facing a fork in the road with no markings in either direction, but having confidence in your choice. Likewise, arriving at an abandoned mine site at the end of a long dirt road is a real thrill—especially when you have all the resources you need to camp in that remote location for an extended period and your future is basically to simply rockhound until you drop. With satellite imagery, downloaded topo maps, GPS coordinates, and basic geology information at your fingertips, you have a real leg up on the old-timers.

CHAPTER 3
HOW TO GET IT HOME

Use this chapter once you have narrowed down your search to a particular thing and an identified area. Your job now is to get to the spot you have picked out and be successful in the field, and there are a lot of modern tools and devices that will help you in your quest.

GETTING TO THE SITE (AND BACK)

One of the joys of rockhounding and prospecting is that most trips into the field begin with a road trip. All the planning and packing finally comes down to getting into a rig and heading out. At this point in the expedition, spirits are high, teams tend to bond, and there is general excitement. If you are an expedition leader or coleader, it is your responsibility to make sure that a great start leads to a great trip all the way through to the end. That means the work is just starting; you cannot

Collecting expeditions are basically road trips with a purpose. Use tubs, totes, and buckets to maintain order.

really relax until you have dropped everyone back off at his or her driveway or car, safe and sound, with great memories, excellent specimens, and no new scars.

There are many ways a caravan or single-vehicle trip can start well and still end badly. You might have a taillight out, which could lead to being pulled over and finding more problems. You might badly need an oil change or tune-up, leading to problems on steep hills. Your tires may be dicey, or your spare might be in bad shape. All of these issues should be taken care of before you get under way.

The following checklist will help you make sure that you are getting started under the best of circumstances.

1. **Engine** tuned up within 5,000 to 10,000 miles of the trip.

2. **Oil** changed within 1,000 to 2,000 miles; all fluids topped off.

3. **Tires** rotated on schedule and spare tire checked. Tire jack and handle functional and complete.

4. **Transmission** checked, flushed within 20,000 miles, and recently topped off with fluid.

5. **Brakes** tested recently; fluid topped off.

6. **Air-conditioning system** tested and topped off. Summer treks to the desert require functioning A/C!

Just checking the main components of your transportation system can save you big headaches out in the backcountry. You should never venture out in a minivan or a sedan onto dicey roads recommended for four-wheel-drive vehicles only. You are not just inviting trouble with clearance issues—you also need a vehicle with a solid suspension system to tackle rutted back roads with mud, rocks, logs, and other obstacles. You might make it home intact, but you would probably have to drive 5 miles an hour or less, with a spotter walking in front of you, to do it.

As the trip leader, it is your responsibility to make sure you have as many safety and repair items as possible. On the next page is a checklist for some additional items that you can toss under the seat in your pickup truck or pack into the spare-tire well in your SUV:

1. **First-aid kit** to handle bug bites, allergic reactions, bee stings, and traumatic injuries. This kit should include some kind of instruction manual.

2. **Tire repair kit.** This includes a puncture repair kit to insert a plug, as well as an air compressor that runs from your cigarette lighter.

Keep a first-aid kit stocked and ready. Make sure your tetanus shot is up to date as well.

3. **Tool kit** of some kind—a set of pliers, a channel-lock, some screwdrivers, and perhaps some sockets.

4. **Roadside assistance kit.** You need flares, reflectors, a vest, and a flashlight for that unthinkable roadside disaster.

You could devote a small tub or box for all the kits if you do not feel the need to tote them back and forth to work every day. However, it is best if these are just part of the vehicle and always in the rig. Auto parts stores carry most of these items; www.autozone.com is one online source.

RVs

Recreational vehicles (RVs) are great for collectors who have earned the opportunity to travel comfortably. If you drive an RV, you already know more than enough to be dangerous. For the purposes of this handbook, the important thing is to keep your vehicle serviced, maintained, and in great operating order. Those who bring a substandard RV into the field will find that they spend most of their time working on the rig while everyone else is off collecting.

Having said that, it is easy to envy a party headed out to the field with an RV towing an SUV or Jeep. The advantage is obvious: Once you park—usually at a campground, RV park, or similar setting, preferably with full hookups—you have all the comforts of home. You will not spend hours setting up a tent, stringing a tarp, or breaking camp at the end of the trip. You will not sleep on the ground, and you will not lack for comfort. You can untether the workhorse vehicle and head out knowing that you are enjoying the best of both worlds.

The disadvantages are obvious: First you need to be close enough to your final destination that you are not spending all your time each day on the road. Second, any time you park around other humans, there is a potential for bad neighbors or other problems. Only you can make the decision about what suits you best. If you are traveling on a route that takes you to the Arkansas diamond locale, to North Carolina's emerald mines, and then up to the fee-dig quartz operation at Herkimer, New York, you might want an RV. If you are headed to a remote part of Idaho where the mountain roads are steep, narrow, and rutted, you might be better off sleeping under the stars.

Trailers

In the same category as RVs, there is a lot to say for a setup where you drive a powerful diesel pickup and tow a luxurious camper to a campground or other reasonable destination. At that point, you untether your main field vehicle and are ready to explore, recon, or otherwise travel.

The disadvantages of parking in an organized campground are the same for RVs and trailers—the potential for bad neighbors, higher expenses, and long commutes to collecting locales. On the other hand, the minimal cost to set up in a state park is not usually a concern for someone consuming dozens of gallons of gas on a weekend.

There are new small, environmentally smart trailers available; check some of them out at www.ScampTrailers.com or www.golittleguy.com. These don't usually require a big V-8 pickup to move around, which is a blessing when you get on small, narrow back roads. The usual workhorse truck is so big that it might not fit in the ruts of the most remote roads, which seem to favor small Jeeps. Driving a big, wide-bodied Hummer H1, for example, on an old mining road means you will be clearing a lot of brush with your paint job.

SUVs

Sport utility vehicles (SUVs) are popular for a reason—they get the job done. Whether you drive a big, long Chevy Suburban or a smaller Subaru Forester, you are in less danger out on the back roads, where clearance and suspension are critical elements.

Having the right vehicle makes those storm clouds a little less intimidating.

The top name in American SUVs is still the Jeep. Go to www.jeep .com and imagine yourself in your own picture.

One consideration when purchasing your next vehicle is ease of repairs. For example, a Lexus SUV with heated seats and climate control may handle the pavement well, and might even do fine on most gravel roads, but if you break down, you are going to have trouble finding the right dealership to get back on the road quickly. You would want to prepare for any trip to an unknown region by making a list of full-service dealerships that can service your luxury vehicle, such as BMW, Mercedes, Lexus, Infiniti, Range Rover, and Hummer.

This advice still holds even for more common US manufacturers such as Ford, Chevy, and Jeep. If you know where the big dealerships are in an area, you can save yourself added expense and wasted time if a breakdown does occur. If you have two vehicles in your party, and one breaks down, at least you know in which direction to go. If you only have one vehicle and must start walking out, at least you can walk in the right direction.

Many remote areas in the western United States still require delivery via Greyhound or Trailways bus for parts shipped from a bigger city.

If you start hearing noises that reflect an expensive repair like a water pump, transmission, or head cover gasket, do not expect an overnight repair.

Depending on the size of your usual group, a small four-person SUV, such as the Jeep Wrangler, might be just what you are looking for. It has a solid suspension, a tight wheelbase, a big gas tank, plenty of storage space, and room for four people without driving them crazy. Smaller SUVs involve trade-offs for cargo and people, and you will want to make sure your clearance is adequate for the back roads or you will end up walking a lot. Still, compared to sedans and minivans, most SUVs are a big step up.

ATVs

One of the best combinations for driving a long distance to a locale and then switching vehicles for intensive recon is to pack an all-terrain vehicle (ATV) in the bed of a pickup. Using this configuration, you do not have to worry about trailers, which can offer more chances for tire damage, more lights to burn out, and more issues when you back up. For a look at a complete setup with a trailer, devised by Oregon gold miner Terry Snider, check out the photo.

PHOTO COURTESY OF TERRY SNIDER

Terry Snider's self-contained setup for a lengthy camp includes an ATV in the bed of the pickup and cooler in the back.

ATVs are one of the great inventions of the past twenty years. They are getting easier and easier to drive, and while prices are not necessarily coming down, the vehicles are fun and fast. If you are older and don't look forward to long hikes, or you want to explore an entire road network, ATVs are the way to go. Just be sure that ATVs are allowed where you'll be traveling. ATVs are prohibited in some areas.

Through interviews and campfire discussions, one name continues to stand out among hunters, rockhounds, prospectors, and others who like to cover a lot of terrain: Bombardier, which you can check out at www.brp.com. BRP, as the company is now known, designs and sells a variety of products, offering such well-known brand names as Ski-Doo, Lynx, Sea-Doo, Evinrude, Johnson, Rotax, and Can-Am. Other enthusiasts swear by Polaris, Honda, Suzuki, and Yamaha. You should have no trouble shopping around on the Internet; Wikipedia has ATV manufacturer links at http://en.wikipedia.org/wiki/All-terrain_vehicle.

In some areas, ATV traffic can churn up a lot of dirt and rock and reveal nice specimens along the trail. In other areas that are gated to normal vehicle traffic, ATVs can reach hard-to-find spots quickly. Access via ATV is not always assured, of course—some gated areas are gated to *all* motor vehicles. It is a good idea to check in with the relevant offices of the USDA Forest Service or BLM and discuss your plans beforehand if you have some big ambitions in remote areas. Always make sure you are up to date on your maps, for example; gates are often marked on the latest travel planning documents.

Snowmobiles

Just as ATVs are handy on poorly maintained back roads, snowmobiles are great for getting around in winter months. It can be a shame to end the collecting season just because of the first snowfall, so something motorized on skis might help you extend the season. The downside is that snow tends to obscure collecting locales, covers creekbeds, and generally gets in the way, so wintertime is usually the season for research and planning.

Tires

It is hard to overestimate the importance of good tires for a safe trip. Standard four-ply tires are quiet on pavement and adequate for most city driving, but out in the field you should consider upgrading your tires to at least eight, if not ten plies. These extra bands of metal fabric help protect your rubber from puncture by rocks, random nails, screws, and bits of steel; the more plies you have, the better.

It pays to establish a relationship with a reputable tire dealer with multiple locales. For example, out in the Pacific Northwest, Les Schwab Tires (www.lesschwab.com) has about 150 tire repair and sales facilities in eight states; they handle brakes, shocks, struts, and alignment. Not only should you leave town with your system in good repair, but it also helps to know where the nearest shop is when you set up camp, in case your friend hasn't read the tire care memo and shows up late with no spare, a bad jack, or no lug nut wrench. The figure on the next page shows a realistic tire repair kit you can include on every trip.

Here is another "Tire Tip" for once you park your vehicle: Beware of metal trash. In many rural areas, campers tend to spend less time cutting and preparing firewood than they used to. They load a flatbed truck with dozens of old wooden pallets and burn those instead. The result is a lot of nails and screws in unlikely places. Be careful when driving anywhere close to a fresh fire ring. If you do end up parking in such an area, try getting one of the kids to drag a powerful magnet on a string or stick around your area and pick up any metal garbage he or she finds. You might be surprised at how many potential disasters you avert in a very short amount of time, and you'll be abiding by the Code of Ethics by leaving a clean camp.

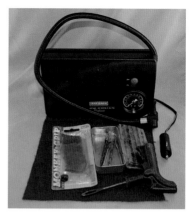
You can tuck an air pump and basic tire repair tools into the well with your spare tire.

Roadside Assistance

You will like the confidence you feel when you strike out into the mountains or desert with a good roadside assistance program at the ready. For anyone with limited car repair skills, this can be especially comforting

Note that once you are out in the wilderness, out of cell phone range, and in a truly remote situation, even the best roadside assistance coverage will not be of immediate help. You'll still have to hike to the nearest community or homestead to reach a landline and call for a tow.

GPS Devices

Cell phones today ship with GPS sensors and built-in mapping programs, and GPS is almost ubiquitous. Many new automobiles sold today have built-in GPS devices from Magellan, Garmin, Tom-Tom, or other vendors. There are also inexpensive dashboard- or windshield-mounted units. Check www.garmin.com for more information on that particular manufacturer's offerings, or check www.tomtom.com for TomTom units or www.magellangps.com for Magellan's devices.

To be truly effective, you usually have to prepare ahead of time with coordinates to enter into the unit. For example, if there is an important turn into a mining district, have your navigator (or whoever is occupying the front seat) standing by to punch in those coordinates. If you rely on just the final coordinates for a locale, the GPS device could suggest a "straighter" but less-traveled road. By entering in the coordinates for your key turns that you identify beforehand, you can prevent the kind of mistake that could prove fatal (more on that later).

Left: The Garmin Oregon 450 works with SD memory cards for state topographic maps.
Right: The Garmin NUVI is a handy navigation tool for the car and will keep even an expert navigator busy.

While GPS devices are a potential godsend if you are driving to a new area you do not know much about, they can be problematic. As the devices become more popular, forest service and BLM personnel have named a new phenomenon: "Death by GPS." It results from motorists blindly following their devices into increasingly dicey road situations and refusing to turn around. Here are two sad stories:

- In 2009 a mother and her son followed their helpful GPS instructions and ended up on a rough desert road in Death Valley; eventually the boy died of exposure.
- In 2011 a Canadian couple traveling from British Columbia to Las Vegas got their Chevy Astro van stuck in the mud. They were out in the Nevada wilderness after taking a "shortcut" identified on their GPS unit. The man left his wife and the rig to seek help and died within 6 miles of town. The woman survived for seven more weeks. A family on ATVs found the man's remains eighteen months later.

The moral of these stories is to use more than one set of data for your planning. We talked about mapping in chapter 2, where we discussed accumulating information beforehand. If you do not want to bring too many maps, you can scan the relevant sections and print them out, creating your own book, as we discussed in chapter 2. Used in conjunction with up-to-date maps and aerial photography, GPS units are a great addition to your arsenal. Just do not trust them solely or above all else.

Gasoline Prices and Availability

We talked earlier about Google Earth layers that you can use to reveal the presence of gas stations. It may not be enough to know that gas is available—you may also want to learn beforehand how much to expect to pay. There are at least three websites that specialize in directing you to the least-expensive fuel options.

GasBuddy

Use Gas Buddy (www.gasbuddy.com) to see where your cheapest options are. On trips where you will be driving a thousand miles round-trip, consuming over fifty gallons of fuel, you can save a lot of money by knowing where to make your stops.

FuelEconomy

Check www.fueleconomy.gov for national trends on gas prices or to check on a certain area. Many states now have pumps open twenty-four hours if you use a credit card, but you don't want to get stuck paying a premium for such a service.

Automotive.com

You can also find low fuel prices and availability at www.automotive .com. From the homepage look under "Tools & Tips > Check Gas Prices."

Cell Coverage

You can search beforehand on cell phone coverage through an area you are about to visit. Your cell phone service provider probably has online maps you can print out. For example, US Cellular provides a coverage map for its subscribers at www.uscellular.com/coverage-map/coverage-indicator.html. Verizon's coverage map is at www.verizonwireless.com/b2c/support/coverage-locator, and AT&T's is at www.wireless.att.com/coverageviewer. You get the idea; you should be able to track down your relevant coverage map without too much effort from here.

You can also use these maps in reverse—figuring out how far you need to go to get the rest and relaxation you need by being unplugged and out of coverage.

Weather

Nothing puts a damper on an expedition like expecting good weather conditions and arriving at your destination in a blizzard, rainstorm, or worse. Fortunately, you can check several websites in the days before you launch.

The Weather Channel operates www.weather.com and offers good information about weather conditions, severe weather warnings, hurricane watches, and more. There are many ads, but the interface is simple to conquer.

Another site to consider is www.weathercentral.com/index.html. You can find links to weather maps, aerial photos, forecasts, hurricane info, and more. You can enter the zip code or the nearest city and state to bring up your forecast.

Weather Underground (www.wunderground.com) also has an easy page to navigate.

If you need international conditions, www.accuweather.com provides both US and international forecasts and reports.

Road Conditions

If you plan a trip during those times of the year when weather conditions can play a big part in your success, you owe it to yourself to check with the state's department of transportation or state highway commission to learn about road conditions. These websites often feature webcams of dicey passes, show road construction, and sometimes even list rest areas. You can search the Internet for "<your state> highway conditions" and quickly navigate to the department of transportation or other state agency you need.

There are national sites as well. For example, Navteq runs www.traffic.com and lets you check traffic conditions for a particular metro area across the United States.

Another site you can check is www.highwayconditions.com for links to conditions in the United States and Canada.

Note that conditions on forest service lands can change quickly due to flooding, washouts, avalanches, environmental studies, wildlife preservation, and more. Check the website of the national forest you plan to visit for updated travel information. Find the telephone number under their Contacts information, and use it.

Radios

When traveling in a single vehicle, your expedition has the advantage of speed and simplicity, but often you will find yourself in, or some-day leading, a caravan of vehicles. The advantage of bringing multiple vehicles is that if anyone suffers a breakdown, there is a backup. The disadvantage is that as the number of vehicles increases, the odds go up that one will experience trouble. One of the first problems is in keeping everyone together.

Small portable radios have limited range but come in handy when your group is splitting into teams or traveling in a caravan.

Although modern cell phones are good for keeping the vehicles in contact, coverage issues can still cause headaches. If you do not have built-in CB radios like the big eighteen-wheel truckers use, the next best solution is to use small, handheld CB radios. Check www.motorola.com for consumer-class two-way radios in a wide range of prices and functionalities. The more you pay, the more likely you are to get solid manufacturing and good signal range. These radios also come in handy when several rockhounds cover a lot of territory, or when a team of prospectors sets out to sample up and down a creek.

There are a couple of issues to keep in mind with handheld radios. It's best if every vehicle in the caravan has a radio tuned to the same frequency, but at the least, make sure the first and last vehicles are equipped. Second, try to make sure you collect all the radios at the end of the expedition. It is pretty easy to turn them off, forget about them, and end up losing them.

Campgrounds

Primitive camping has its charms. The solitude of a remote locale is soothing, and less traffic means fewer neighbors. Dry camping (no water) is definitely a challenge—most campers would prefer to at least have water nearby that they can boil or filter, and the sound of rushing water is relaxing. But if you are comfortable with bringing your own water and rationing it carefully, you can have a great experience in remote locales right where you plan to collect. And there may be a lot fewer bugs.

At the other end of the spectrum, organized campgrounds boast obvious advantages. Even having a picnic table can be a great upgrade, and clean running water comes in handy. More conveniences mean more dollars and, again, more neighbors, but the cost can be worth it. And you may sometimes have to accommodate those who prefer more upgrades than you yourself require. While many state and national campgrounds remain "first come, first served," it is comforting to drive for eight hours to a remote campground and *know* that you have a reserved spot. Consider the links below for more information.

Free Camping
http://freecampsites.net

Good interactive map lets you pinpoint free camping areas near your destination. The site also includes pay campgrounds, and you can search fairly easily. The site uses the icons for water, swimming areas, etc., to provide more information. Users can submit a site as well.

Campgrounds.com
www.campgrounds.com

Very extensive, with believable reviews and plenty of feedback.

Reserve America
www.reserveamerica.com

Good for reservations. Nice search feature.

Go Camping
www.gocampingamerica.com

Not as extensive as other sites.

Recreation.gov
www.recreation.gov

Especially good for reserving spots at government campsites.

KOA
www.koa.com

KOA has a great nationwide network.

RV Camping
www.rv-camping.org

Good interactive map; solid spot for RVers.

In addition to the campgrounds listed at these websites, there are numerous county and state parks, many of which host overnight camping; some take reservations. Expand your search as needed.

If you do not have a lot of flexibility and are really depending on a campground being open, you definitely must contact the relevant agency or organization. Many sites take reservations online now. If you are planning to visit a campground maintained by the USDA Forest Service that does not have reservable spots, you should look it up on the relevant forest service website but also contact them via e-mail or phone. Conditions change constantly in the forest—intense winter storms can wash out roads, bridges, and entire campgrounds. Forest fires can shut down immense areas. Controlled burns, presale thinning, road and culvert repairs, fish rehabilitation, and even escaped convicts can all interfere with your plans.

Note too that just because you saw a campground listed on Google Earth or on GeoCommunicator's topographic maps is no guarantee the campground is still in service.

It helps to have a main plan and a backup plan. If the campground you are counting on turns out to be full when you arrive after midnight, you need a Plan B. Can you easily backtrack to a dispersed camping site? Keep in mind that during peak vacation periods, such as Memorial Day, Fourth of July, and Labor Day, you could be hard-pressed to find even a good primitive spot unless you arrive very early. Similarly, if you are venturing out in springtime in an area that has seen dramatic flooding, all the normal sites along the water will be gone, pushing all campers to investigate their own Plan B or even Plan C.

GENERAL FIELDWORK POINTERS

So far, all the advice in this chapter has been on getting you to a certain locale. Now comes the hard part: working. Here again, the revolution in modern tools and equipment can be particularly helpful.

In a 2012 article from *Science Daily*, geologists talked about how their world has changed for the better.

Nov. 5, 2012—Not very long ago a professional geologist's field kit consisted of a Brunton compass, rock hammer, magnifying glass, and field notebook. No longer. In the field and in the labs and classrooms, studying Earth has undergone an explosive change in recent years, fueled by technological leaps in handheld digital devices, especially tablet computers and cameras.

Geologist Terry Pavlis' digital epiphany came almost 20 years ago when he was in a museum looking at a 19th-century geology exhibit that included a Brunton compass. 'Holy moly!' he remembers thinking, 'We're still using this tool.' This is despite the fact that technological changes over the last 10 years have not only made the Brunton compass obsolete, but swept away paper field notebooks as well (the rock hammer and hand-lens magnifier remain unchallenged, however).

The key technologies that replace the 19th-century field tools are the smart phone, PDA, handheld GPS, and tablet PC and iPad. Modern tablets, in particular, can do everything a Brunton compass can, plus take pictures and act as both a notebook and mapping device, and gather precise location data using GPS. They can even be equipped with open-source GIS software."

[Source: Geological Society of America (2012, November 5). "Field geologists (finally) going digital." *ScienceDaily*. Retrieved December 29, 2012, from www.sciencedaily.com/releases/2012/11/121105100928.htm]

You may not need most of those devices, and the hand lens and rock hammer will still be key tools. It is still nice to know the revolution has arrived.

Code of Ethics

Before going any further, you need to understand your rights and responsibilities as you pursue geological specimens in the field. Due to trouble over the years with unscrupulous collectors, overzealous beginners, inexperienced campers, poor drivers, and messy humans, there is a large body of evidence that supports the idea that we can be better stewards of public land. The American Federation of Mineralogical Societies has developed a Code of Ethics to help guide everyone so they understand their duties; it is published at www.amfed.org/ethics.htm.

Help spread the word, and be a responsible citizen out there. Our continued access to public lands depends on you!

Code of Ethics

I will respect both private and public property and will do no collecting on privately owned land without permission from the owner.

I will keep informed on all laws, regulations or rules governing collecting on public lands and will observe them.

I will, to the best of my ability, ascertain the boundary lines of property on which I plan to collect.

I will use no firearms or blasting material in collecting areas.

I will cause no willful damage to property of any kind such as fences, signs, buildings, etc.

I will leave all gates as found.

I will build fires only in designated or safe places and will be certain they are completely extinguished before leaving the area.

I will discard no burning material—matches, cigarettes, etc.

I will fill all excavation holes which may be dangerous to livestock.

I will not contaminate wells, creeks, or other water supplies.

I will cause no willful damage to collecting material and will take home only what I can reasonably use.

I will practice conservation and undertake to utilize fully and well the materials I have collected and will recycle my surplus for the pleasure and benefit of others.

I will support the rockhound project H.E.L.P. (Help Eliminate Litter Please) and will leave all collecting areas devoid of litter, regardless of how found.

I will cooperate with field-trip leaders and those in designated authority in all collecting areas.

I will report to my club or federation officers, Bureau of Land Management or other authorities, any deposit of petrified wood or other materials on public lands which should be protected for the enjoyment of future generations for public educational and scientific purposes.

I will appreciate and protect our heritage of natural resources.

I will observe the "Golden Rule," will use good outdoor manners and will at all times conduct myself in a manner which will add to the stature and public image of rockhounds everywhere.

[Revised July 7, 1999 at the AFMS Annual Meeting]

Clothing

Old-time prospectors had it rough; first they had to get a balky mule into the mountains with all their gear, and then they had primitive tools to work with. They used gold pans with no riffles, for example, and would have greatly appreciated a backpack dredge setup. So modern rockhounds and prospectors not only have much better transportation into the collecting locale but also have far better tools and gear.

When you first start out collecting geological treasures, you may think nothing of exploring in short pants and sneakers with an adult beverage in one hand as you stray barely beyond earshot of the vehicle. Sometimes the enthusiasm of finally reaching your destination is just too hard to resist, and you may find yourself under-equipped. Experienced field workers know that once they park and turn the engine off, the work is only just beginning, and it is important to be prepared.

For example, consider protective clothing, as shown in the photo. If you purchase a solid set of coveralls such as from Carhartt (www .carhartt.com), you will protect your better clothing while your rugged coveralls absorb the most abuse from sharp rocks, tools, etc. You don't always envision yourself crawling on boulders, working from your elbows, or many of the other difficult positions you can find yourself in.

Smart rockhounds wear coveralls to protect their clothes.

It is nice to return to the campsite after a long day, peel off your dirty coveralls, and be somewhat clean and ready to cook. Likewise, trashing that new sweatshirt you got for Father's Day could get you in trouble with the gift-giver.

Several manufacturers make waterproof gear for serious creek work, although they usually market to anglers and hunters, or even construction workers, rather than rockhounds. On a handful of warm summer days, having an expensive set of waterproof waders is overkill, but most of the time, and especially in spring and fall, when the water and the air temperature stay cold or cool, you'll get a lot more done with the right equipment.

It is best to avoid cotton clothing. Rescue teams and Explorer Scouts have a saying based on years of rescuing ill-equipped city folks out in the woods: "Cotton kills." Blue jeans are great for summer days where you only have to worry about keeping the brush from shredding your shins. Once you start to encounter any kind of moisture, however, cotton is quick to get wet and slow to dry off. Wool and modern synthetics are far superior to cotton if you run into rain or snow. That is really the best advice you need: Do not rely on your jeans if the weather is cold or wet. You are at serious risk of hypothermia if you are wearing only cotton. Go for a layered approach with good, modern outdoor gear that wicks away moisture and is easy to wring out.

You are on your own for footwear, as your mileage will certainly vary depending on your disposable cash, attitude toward old shoes, and tendency to over-pack. Shoes are an easy item to indulge in because the pay-off is high. For example, cheap rubber boots are great for keeping your feet dry but hard to walk in for any distance; high-end waterproof boots might be better for you. Sometimes a pair of crummy old sneakers or sandals is the perfect shoe for walking in creeks and looking for agates; you can simply recycle them or toss them in a Dumpster when done. An expensive set of boots is not always the best bet, even though the tread might come in handy crossing slippery rocks. Many miners who work with heavy hammers and move lots of rock refuse to work in anything that does not have steel toes, which is smart advice for rockhounds too.

Even more important might be the right kind of wool or polypropylene socks, which can be wrung dry and reused quickly. Again, avoid cotton. Take advantage of the modern fabrics from Columbia Sportswear (www.columbia.com), for example, where they sell all kinds of modern, high-tech gear that breathes, reflects, wicks, shields, and blocks.

Online Outfitters

There are dozens of outdoor equipment sellers with ¿
L.L.Bean (www.llbean.com) comes to mind. Cabela's (w
has great gear to choose from, as do REI (www.rei.com) ¿
(www.backcountry.com). Bass Pro (www.basspro.com) has a wi͟͟
tory, and Eddie Bauer has outlet stores at many malls. Their website
is www.eddiebauer.com. Other outfitter sites include www.patagonia
.com, www.MountainGear.com, www.landsend.com, and www.Campmore
.com.

Army-Navy Surplus

Having listed all the top-dollar stores, you might get much better deals
at the modern equivalent of an Army-Navy surplus store. One national
site is www.armynavysales.com, which offers an excellent inventory.
Another spot is Major Surplus (www.majorsurplus.com). There may be a
local store near you to check as well. You can perform a simple Internet
search to find a surplus store you can visit in person and try on clothing
before you purchase.

Tools

Now let's talk about tools.

Hand Lens

Field geologists and accomplished prospectors use a hand lens constantly
to check for crystals, tiny fossils, and more. Refer to the figure for a selection you can choose from. Your ability to identify common rock-forming
minerals, for example, will assist you in many ways. A hand lens is usually inexpensive, especially considering the value it provides.

- **Rockhounds** use a hand lens to determine if they are seeing quartz
  or calcite by approximating the angles of the crystal faces they see.
- **Gold panners** use a hand lens to inspect black sands for garnets,
  minute particles of gold, and other clues.
- **Fossil diggers** use a hand lens to inspect leaves for cell
  structure, search limestone for tiny fossil skeletons, and view
  foraminifera—small, microscopic fossils not always obvious to
  the naked eye.
- **Meteorite hunters** use a hand lens to check for a fusion crust,
  evidence of flow lines, and other clues.

ausch & Lomb makes a ssic 7x to 20x Hastings trip-let, similar to the tool shown in the photo, that should be more than enough tool for you. A hand lens is an easy tool to find online; one good source is Kooter's Geology Tools (http://kooters .com). Another site with a wide selection is The Compleat Natu-ralist (www.compleatnaturalist .com/Catalog_Category_pages/ magnifiers.htm).

REQUIRED TOOL! Use a hand lens or loupe to inspect crystal faces, check black sands for garnets, peer at mystery rocks, and more.

Rock Hammers

You need at least one good geology pick in your ham-mer collection to call your-self a rockhound. The classic hammer is the blue-handled Estwing product with the pointed tip, which is a fine entry-level tool. Chances are that the more you get out into the field, and the more you

It is hard to know when to stop collecting hammers and chisels—they are an important part of your fieldwork.

find yourself supplying "loaners" to young Scouts, family friends, and others in your caravan, the more you will be tempted to experiment with designs, features, and sizes. Eventually you may end up with a collection of tools similar to those shown here.

As shown in the photo and described in Table 3, Estwing has an impressive collection of differ-ent geology hammers and tools, available at www.estwing.com/ geological_tools.php.

Estwing carries an excellent assortment of geological tools. Collect them all! Courtesy of Eastwing

Table 3: Estwing Hammers and Their Features and Uses

Hammer Feature	Consideration
Pointed tip	Good for expanding crevices, chipping out concretions, and digging out veins and cracks.
Chisel tip	Best for splitting shales and sedimentary rocks to reveal fossil leaves.
Square head	Larger striking face delivers more force to an area.
Long handle	Safer distance from impact means fewer rock chips against your knuckles. Harder to swing for kids, women, and the elderly.
Blue, cushioned handle	Better shock-resistance; less chance for stinging hands after long use.
Leather handle	Better looking; classic for professionals.
Hammer Types	
Big Blue	Also known as a bricklayer or mason's hammer. Square head and chisel end, cushioned handle. Good control for precise chipping and fashioning.
Chipping Hammer	Vertical chisel end used to fashion tiles; a pointed tip; cushioned handle. Delivers precise force to small area.
Geo/Paleo Pick	4 pounds, 25 inches; pointed end and chisel edge; cushioned grip. Excellent for tearing apart sedimentary rock exposures.
Crack Hammer	2–4 pounds, 10.5–11 inches; cushioned handle; two polished faces. Also comes in 4-pound, 16-inch, long-handled version. Best tool for breaking down large specimens, including igneous and metamorphic rocks.
Engineer's Hammer	48 ounces, 16 inches; two polished faces. Longer, cushioned handle for protection from flying chips.
Cross Peen Hammer	24–40 ounces, 13–14.25 inches; cushioned grip, flat hammer face and blunt chisel end. Excellent for reducing hand samples, attacking tailings piles, and driving chisels.

Ultraviolet Lamps

Fluorescence refers to the ability of black light to bounce ions out of their comfort level and make minerals appear a different color. Most of us have seen how certain minerals, such as calcite, exhibit fluorescence and glow in the dark. There are both short- and long-wave ultraviolet lights. Either of the two UV lamps shown

Ultraviolet lights (also known as black lights) are used to test fluorescence.

here would be a valuable addition to your gear. The top lamp is more expensive but features both long and short waves. The bottom lamp is cheaper—and easier to use.

Did you know that scorpions fluoresce under ultraviolet light? Check for yourself the next time you are out in the Western desert at night.

Geiger Counters

At one time there was a serious uranium rush in the Western states, but excitement quickly waned after the mid-1950s. Once US stockpiles were adequate for the Cold War, and most of the concentrated uranium was discovered and exploited, serious uranium prospecting tailed off dramatically. When the government was enthusiastic about locating new deposits, however, it was common to see young men out in the field with primitive Geiger counters, hoping for the loud chatter of a hot zone.

Nowadays you are just as likely to purchase a radiation detector to see if your home is building up radon gas. After the 2011 Fukushima disaster in Japan, there was an uptick in radiation detector sales. Mazur Instruments sells a nice one for $600 at www.mazurinstruments.com.

If you want to really dig deep in the technology behind radiation detection, check out this link and shake your head in disbelief at the rockhounds smoking cigars while they mess with radioactive rocks: http://blog.modernmechanix.com/how-to-choose-a-geiger-counter.

Screens

Every type of geological specimen collector should need a screen at one time or another:

1. **Rockhounds.** Screens are great for small crystals such as garnets, quartz, tourmaline, and staurolite. If the ground is dry, you can screen crystals from the dust. Otherwise you can screen material in the creek.

2. **Fossil collectors.** Screens can help when you are looking for snails replaced by chalcedony, or when you are searching for small concretions in a sandy beach.

3. **Gold prospectors.** Screens help classify material, remove larger rocks and cobbles, and help you prepare your concentrates for machine cleaning.

4. **Meteorite hunters.** Screens help around an impact site to accumulate meteorite fragments buried in the sand.

Several manufacturers supply rugged screens of all sizes and shapes. Keene Engineering Company (www.keeneeng.com) is one worth remembering. However, you can make do with any rugged, used kitchen screens you spot at garage sales and second-hand stores. See if you can guess which screens in the accompanying figure did not come from a prospecting shop.

Assortment of screens for any number of jobs

Sample Bags and Jars

When you are just starting out, you may be content to fill your pockets with pretty rocks and check them at the end of the day. But as you find more material, and get more scientific about your searches, you are going to want to use sample jars, specimen bags, and make notes to yourself.

One of the easiest ways to keep track of your specimens on a busy field day is to use a plastic bag with a zipper-style closure. If you have some old business cards that are printed on very sturdy stock, you can jot down your notes on the blank backsides of the cards with a fine-tip, permanent-ink felt pen and slide the cards right in with your specimens. If you don't write with large letters you'll have room for GPS coordinates and other field notes.

Otherwise you might want to pick up a field notebook. These were very common back in the day but could get beat up after a few trips. And to tell the truth, paper and pencil is old-school thinking. You're probably better off just having someone film a quick video of you, your finds, and some important notes.

Prospectors who wash gravel for gold, platinum, diamonds, or garnets may find themselves needing several sample jars to keep material straight. Sampling from multiple locations can mean you need to pick up a bunch of jars and bottles, such as those shown below.

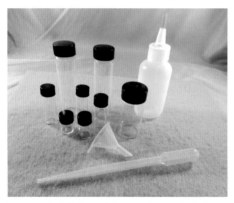
Fine assortment of sample jars won in a contest at www.GoldProspectorsspace.com

Assortment of filled sample jars, waiting for a quiet afternoon in the off-season

Plastic trays or boxes with dividers also make for a nice field tool. If you are collecting anything fragile, such as fossil leaves, obsidian needles, or mica chunks, a plastic box with a lid can come in very handy. Make sure you have enough tissue or paper towels to stuff inside for extra protection.

Be sure to label your jars, even with simple white tape and permanent markers.

Other Tools

Many rockhounds find that they need chisels and pry bars, and they brag about their carbide-tipped chisels. Gold prospectors also need pry bars on occasion to move boulders in the creek and want the longest possible bar for greater leverage. Paleontologists often use bladed tools to break open shale or sandstone in search of leaves. Check at Harbor Freight, Estwing, or other sites. Some typical tools are shown here.

Brushes such as those shown here are helpful for all geological specimen collectors:

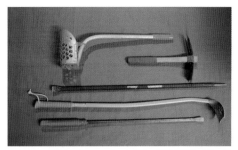

Some typical field tools. From the top: a coarse scoop for gravel, a combo handpick, a pointed bar, a "back-saver" rockhound scoop, a "super screwdriver."

Safety tip: Goggles are cheap compared to the pain of a wounded eye.

- **Rock and gem collectors** use stiff brushes to remove dirt and mud from specimens.
- **Gold panners** use stiff brushes to clean out crevices.
- **Fossil diggers** use softer brushes to wipe off fossil-bearing outcrops.
- **Meteorite hunters** use brushes to remove rust from iron-rich specimens.

As a final note on tools, there is currently a $10 million contest under way to develop the equiva-

Brushes are handy for all collectors, whether removing mud, sand, dust, or rust.

lent of a *Star Trek* tricorder. Currently the prize is for the medical equivalent, not for determining the amount of plagioclase feldspars in the rocks around you. You can do an Internet search if this link doesn't work:

http://mobihealthnews.com/19601/with-final-guidelines
-tri corder-x-prize-is-on.

If you ever watched Commander Spock working the legendary Tricorder device while fulfilling his duties as Science Officer, you can imagine how helpful it could be to your rockhounding and prospecting efforts. Unfortunately, such a device is still several years away.

CHAPTER 4
WORKING IN THE FIELD

Use this chapter to increase your chances of success collecting rocks and minerals out in the field.

OCEAN BEACHES

Some of the easiest and most relaxing rockhounding you can ever do is to walk along an ocean beach, head down, and pick up interesting material. The Pacific Northwest ocean beaches are ideal for collecting agate, jasper, petrified wood, fossils, and other interesting material. Often this tumbler material can skip the first three stages and go right to polishing.

The only real trick to rockhounding beach gravels is to mind the tides and the seasons. The worst possible time would be summer at high tide. Not only have the waves slacked off and stopped moving sand around, the water will cover everything else. Plus the crowds are bigger, as you can see in the photo on the next page, showing a popular Oregon locale. If you only have one shot at success, you want to time your visit for the stormy season and a significant low tide. If you can get those two variables controlled, you should be fine. However, you can see from the images on the next two pages that there are very few bad days at the beach.

One good place to check for online tide tables is the website of the National Oceanic and Atmospheric Administration (NOAA): http://tides andcurrents.noaa.gov. Click through to their Tides & Currents page and you can create a PDF of the full year's tidal predictions. There are probably some sophisticated ways to save their data and search for interesting tides in the -1.5 or lower range, but that is only applicable if you have a lot of time in your schedule and can drop everything to rush to the coast for the lowest tides.

Note that stormy conditions at the beach can interfere with your success. Collectors usually already have good rain gear and boots, hats and gloves, and other comfortable clothing. One additional piece of gear to consider might be goggles to keep your eyes free of mist, sand, and salty air. (Goggles are covered in more depth in the "Desert Walks" section.)

Popular agate collecting beds at Gleneden Beach, south of Lincoln City, Oregon

Atlantic Ocean beaches, such as this one in northern New Jersey, have plenty of quartzite, chalcedony, and tumble-polished metamorphic rocks to collect.

This gravel bar on the northern New Jersey coast has plenty of material ready for the tumbler.

Legal Issues

Petrified wood. The collection of petrified wood is governed by state and federal regulations. Persons may collect petrified wood from public lands for noncommercial purposes without charge. There is a limit of 25 pounds per person per day, plus one piece (to avoid breaking a large piece), to a maximum of 250 pounds per year.

Artifacts. Virtually all sources of colored silica (agate, chalcedony, jasper, obsidian, etc.) have been historically used by Native Americans in the building of weapons and other tools. The collection of any artifacts, including projectile points, ovate bifaces, cores, flakes, and all other material worked by prehistoric cultures and now found on public lands, is prohibited by the Antiquities Act of 1906 and the Archaeological Resources Protection Act of 1979 without an archaeological permit. Such permits may be obtained from BLM state offices.

Note that such permits are rarely, if ever, issued. Your best bet is to join a club, as Gator Girl suggested in chapter 1. Check this link for more information about archeology clubs: http://archaeology.about.com/od/associations/Associations _and_Clubs_in_Archaeology.htm.

Decorative rock. With respect to the collecting of decorative veneer stone, BLM field offices consider a "reasonable quantity" to be not more than can be carried in the trunk of a car.

Following is a handy guide for some techniques and hunting tips at the beach.

Agates
Walk so that the sun is in front of you, and try to get the angle of the sunbeams positioned so that agates seem to fill with light. There are numerous types of agate—banded, fortification, mossy, etc., but they are often very small by the time they reach the ocean. Your best bet is to find areas with basalt flows nearby, where the agates might be eroding directly from nearby formations rather than transported via rivers and currents.

Jasper/Chert/Flint
Look for shiny surfaces when wet, but check to see if the surface appears dull and porous when dried off. Only the hardest materials take a good polish. See if you can spot the characteristic shell-shaped, conchoidal fracture of a hard cryptocrystalline quartz that a flint knapper would appreciate.

Most common jasper is tan or yellow. Red is common on some beaches; green is usually rare. Chert is often red. Flint is often dull gray.

Petrified Wood
Look for parallel lines, a sure way to spot petrified wood. Most chunks at least show some woody structure. Fresh petrified wood is usually tan or yellow, but with replacement, iron can intrude and stain the rock dark brown or black. Petrified wood is often confused with hardened mudstones, siltstones, and sandstones that also show parallel lines but are usually softer. Schists usually show too much swirling to consider as petrified wood.

Quartzite
Quartzite is a hard type of quartz-rich rock that usually reveals clues about the way it was originally laid down when it was a sandstone. It has been cooked and hardened considerably, but it takes a good polish and is attractive even when solid white. Often a creamy yellow or tan, it ranges to reddish, orange, and yellow.

Chalcedony
Chalcedony is a catchall term for many varieties of quartz. If you find a rock with a hardness of 7 but not very translucent, and certainly not an

agate, it might be properly termed chalcedony. Chalcedony often has a creamy white appearance and sometimes appears banded.

Metamorphic Rocks
Some forms of gneiss are very hard and take a nice polish. Harder schists do, as well.

Fossils
Finding fossils at the beach involves either digging them out of cliffs and rocks or finding concretions with fossil material inside. Many, if not most, popular beaches have severe restrictions against digging into cliffs and speeding up erosion. You are safer to look for round concretions that have begun to erode and reveal a shell or tooth inside. Since the fossilized shell material is harder than the surrounding concretion, you can find shell, tooth, or even bone starting to protrude from a round concretion.

Other Materials
Tumble-polished granites sometimes look quite nice, especially when completely round or oval.

Oregon Agates
If you have never searched for agates along the Oregon coast, you are missing a treat. Here is a link to Agates of the Oregon Coast: www.agates oftheoregoncoast.com. Operators K. T. Myers and Richard Petrovic sell a handy laminated, full-color pocket guide for coastal treasures, both in the rough state and once polished.

CREEK AND RIVER WALKS
Gravel bars along creeks and rivers are fantastic resources to check for interesting tumbler material. Depending on the size and variety of rocks in the drainage area, these walks can be very rewarding. Many of the same rules apply that were important while beachcombing. You need to mind the angle of the sun, preferably keeping it in front of you, to spot agates easily. Petrified wood has characteristic lines, and you only want the hardest, shiniest jaspers.

Creeks and rivers often carry much rougher material that has sometimes only moved slightly from its source. Longer river systems such as the Columbia, Missouri, and Mississippi move material thousands of miles, but they are the exception. Many creeks may only move material 20 miles or so, and most of the rough edges may still be present. That usually means slightly more time in the tumbler at the coarsest grit, but material sizes are much bigger.

This scenic gravel bar on the Clearwater River near Elk City, Idaho, is full of such collectibles as gold, garnet, chalcedony, and jasper.

Like ocean beach collecting, you need low water to guara[?] most success for a creek or river walk. This usually means July, and September are your best options, but be flexible. There a[?] years in which January and February have dramatically low water levels, and if you can stand the temperature, you may have much better luck. If there is a particular area you are thinking of checking, you may also want to keep an eye on the weather, such as through www.weather.com, to see if any rainstorms have moved through that area.

It sometimes feels as though all the best gravel bars are on the "wrong" side of the creek or river. One way to get around that is with a Ski-doo, kayak, or canoe, such as in the image shown here.

A canoe or kayak trip during low water can help you access areas that rarely see collectors.

Two online resources can help greatly in your search for creek and river gravels. First you can use Google Maps or Google Earth to track a watercourse's path through aerial photography and spot likely targets. If you can find dramatic expanses of gravels just waiting to be inspected, then you only need to figure out a way to get there. Refer back to chapter 2 for more information about Google Earth. Next we will look at water level research.

Water Levels

Use the USGS's water levels page to see how your targeted water drainage system is faring as far as runoff conditions are concerned. Check their interactive map at http://waterdata.usgs.gov/nwis/rt. You will pull up a graphic such as the one in the accompanying figure. As you study an area and wait for the right conditions, you may find yourself torn between two conditions: hoping for nasty storms to churn up the gravels and give you a shot at new stuff, and rooting for drought conditions that reveal long-lost gravel exposures not hunted in years.

Practical tip: Make sure you do not root for either floods or droughts aloud, within earshot of ranchers and farmers.

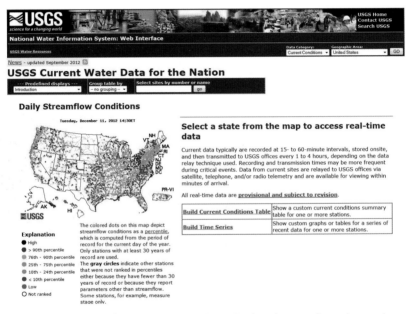

A look at the USGS's water data page will tell you if water levels are low enough to make a creek walk worthwhile.

Once you have targeted an area and know what to expect for water levels, you can set about accessing the gravels.

State Access Programs

One of the best trends for rockhounds in general is the development of designated access sites to rivers and creeks through state departments of fish and wildlife. In Idaho this is known as the "Access—Yes!" program. Washington and Oregon have followed suit, as have most other

Western states. If you search on your state name and "fishing access," you should find what you need. For example, for "Nevada fishing access" you will find a link to the Nevada Department of Wildlife and an interactive map at http://ndow.org/fish/where/index.shtm.

If you want to search for material in Nebraska, you could search on "Nebraska fishing access" and would get a link to http://outdoornebraska .ne.gov/fishing/guides/fishguide/FGwaters.asp. The site is searchable and easy to use. Rockhounds owe anglers a debt of gratitude for making easy, legal access to the water a priority.

Note: The downside to these growing state programs is that there may come a time when you are required to have a general-use permit to rockhound on these sites if you do not carry a fishing license. Hopefully it will be worth it.

While it is uncommon to find camping available at these state sites, you will often find good parking, a nice trail to the water, and perhaps a picnic table, garbage can, and outhouse.

The model more states should follow is that of the Washington Department of Fish and Wildlife (see http://wdfw.wa.gov/lands/water_

access). These folks list the GPS coordinates and often show pictures of the site.

Check to see if your state has initiated a similar program for access to popular fishing spots.

Material such as shown in the photo can be a good reward for a cold, wet creek walk. As noted earlier, pieces are usually larger, having moved less distance.

Dramatic red jaspers, shiny orange carnelian, and decent petrified wood from a walk along Salmon Creek, Washington

DESERT WALKS

Many of the problems you face with planning rockhounding trips along ocean beaches, rivers, and creeks do not apply to desert walks. There are no tides to plan for, and since most US deserts are on BLM land, you will not have the big access issues. Of course some famous deserts have a different challenge: Death Valley National Monument, for example, like all national parks and monuments, is closed to collecting.

While too much water is rarely a big issue in the desert, it can be a nuisance when it shows up. Some roads in dry climates turn into a thick, slippery gumbo when saturated. Even a four-wheel-drive vehicle can have difficulty staying on the road under wet conditions. There are also washouts, flash floods, and other calamities to account for. Some beginning rockhounds only compound their problems by driving in places where their rig was never meant to go, such as across the playa during a rainstorm.

Desert terrain typical of the western Basin and Range country

Weather Concerns

One way around these issues is to keep an eye on your favorite weather-reporting site. If you're planning to search a specific area, you can also surf to the web pages of a local newspaper. For example, one spring in southwest Idaho, there were so many off-road vehicles getting stuck out in the sagebrush hills that the local towing company finally cried "uncle" and asked the BLM and forest service to close a few of the more popular, and treacherous, roads until the area dried out. The local newspaper reported on the closures.

Fire Danger

The Active Fire Mapping Program (http://activefiremaps.fs.fed.us) lists the current large fires that can impact your collecting plans. By June most desert climates have burned off the bulk of their spring moisture. By the Fourth of July, restrictions start to take effect. Usually the first thing to go is your ability to build a campfire outside of organized campgrounds. You can usually still use charcoal or propane. By the end of July, even that is usually out of the question, but you can still use propane in a campground. By August some areas are locked up, and you can't even access the lands. Before you head out to public lands, check with the local BLM or forest service office to find out what conditions are in effect. Here's a typical progression:

Stage 1

The following acts are prohibited:

1. Building, maintaining, attending, or using a fire or campfire except within a developed recreation site, or improved site.

2. Smoking, except within an enclosed vehicle or building, a developed recreation site, or while stopped in an area at least 3 feet in diameter that is barren or cleared of all flammable materials.

3. Operating or using any internal or external combustion engine without a spark-arresting device properly installed, maintained, and in effective working order.

Stage 2

The following acts are prohibited, in addition to the prohibitions of Stage 1:

1. Building, maintaining, attending, or using a fire or campfire.

2. Smoking, except within an enclosed vehicle or building.

3. Possessing, discharging, or using any kind of firework or other pyrotechnic device.

4. Using an explosive.

5. Operating a chainsaw or other equipment powered by an internal combustion engine between 1 p.m. and 1 a.m.

6. Operating or using any internal or external combustion engine without a spark-arresting device properly installed, maintained, and in effective working order

7. Welding or operating an acetylene or other torch with open flame.

8. Possess or use a motor vehicle off forest system roads, except when parking in an area devoid of vegetation within 10 feet of the roadway.

Stage 3

The area is closed to all entry except for limited access for landowners and other rare instances.

Water

You can survive the desert heat if you find shade and bring sufficient water. You obviously cannot count on finding much water in the desert, but if you do, you have to treat it before you drink it. There are many common parasites and other organisms in untreated water that will make you sick if you drink it. You would be smart to invest in a water filtration system of some kind; at least carry a small bottle of water purification tablets tucked away in a survival kit. Visit www.bepreparedtosurvive .com/WaterPurificationProducts.htm for more information.

Sunscreen

Bring your wide-brimmed hat and cover up. If you wear a baseball-style cap, you expose your ears and the back of your neck to the hot sun all day. You should always dress appropriately and make a big deal out of using sunscreen. Skin cancer is a very real threat to anyone who spends time in the desert's baking heat. You will know the team is taking it seriously when a good, healthy competition breaks out as to who is using the highest SPF-rated sunscreen. Try to win that competition.

Eye Protection

One tip you might not have considered is to protect your eyes. Since you rely on your vision to spot collectibles, think about investing in some high-end goggles. Wraparound sunglasses are fine for much of the time, but when the wind kicks up and your eyes constantly form tears, your treasure count is going to suffer.

For example, at www.wileyx.com you can find safety goggles that meet military specifications for ballistic impact, ventilate from the top, and look formidable, but they cost over $100; check www.wileyx.com/Ecomm Suite/ProductListing.aspx?ActivityCode=SAFETY&SeriesCode=800.

Those are very high end in price, however. At www.armynavydeals .com you can find a wide assortment of what are known as "tanker goggles" or "Rommel goggles" that should work just fine.

Vehicle Care

Finally, your trip into the desert is wholly reliant on the health o
vehicle. As covered earlier, make sure you have the right rig for the job
and that all your key maintenance and upkeep chores are complete. You're
A/C system is going to get a lot of use—check it before you go. You should
probably pack some extra water in case your vehicle's engine cooling
system acts up. Sharper rocks put more pressure on old, thin tires.

With those threats covered, let's talk about the good news. Desert rockhounding is often much more successful because there is so little vegetation to obscure rock outcrops. Meteorites and fossils last much longer
in dry conditions. Creeks and gullies tend to see violent, turbulent flooding, which breaks up material and exposes outcrops. The long-angled
rays of the sun at the beginning and end of each day are like candy for
photographers; there are usually enough wildlife shots, impressive vis-
tas and terrains, old, crumbling buildings, and other dramatic composi-
tions to keep everyone happy.

Desert Astronomy

Night in the desert brings tremendous stargazing opportunities. There are
far fewer light sources to mar your view of the skies, so light pollution is not
usually an issue. Out in the desert you can usually get a nice panorama of all
horizons, so you will see planets come into view in the east and travel across
the southern sky to set in the west. You will spot traveling satellites, the
International Space Station (ISS), and perhaps even the Hubble telescope.

Here is a link to set you up for tracking the ISS: www.ehow.com/
how_4861131_international-space-station-night-sky.html.

Check Sky and Telescope (www.skyandtelescope.com/observing/
skychart) for sky charts and tons of information about when planets
and the moon rise and set. For example, just before you head out of town
you can check their continually updated "This Week's Sky at a Glance"
page (www.skyandtelescope.com/observing/ataglance) to make sure you
do not miss the important stuff.

One trick for combining the best of astronomy and desert rockhounding is to time your visit to coincide with well-known meteor showers.
The best summer meteor shower is usually the Perseid shower, which
peaks around August 12 each year. There are numerous showers to work
with, however. The Saguaro Astronomy Club has a comprehensive list at
www.saguaroastro.org/content/ANNUALmeteorSHOWERS.htm.

Here are some of the highlights for a recent year. The showers occur at roughly the same time annually, but the actual dates will shift around, so check the site for your needs:

Table 4: Popular Meteor Shower Dates to Consider When Rockhounding in the Desert

Name	Dates	Peak	#/hr	Rating
Quantrantids	Jan 1–5	Jan 3	120	bright
Lyrids	Apr 16–Apr 25	Apr 22	18	bright
Eta Aquarids	Apr 19–May 28	May 5	65	bright
Arietids	May 22–July 2	June 7	54	bright
Perseids	July 17–Aug 24	Aug 12	100	bright
Orionids	Oct 2–Nov 7	Oct 21	25	bright
Leonids	Nov 14–Nov 21	Nov 17	15	bright
Geminids	Dec 7–Dec 17	Dec 13	120	medium

Desert Links

You are not alone if you enjoy the solitude and challenge of the desert. Here is a list of some popular desert rockhounding websites.

DzrtGrls

www.dzrtgrls.com

Awesome explorers. Click their "Trips" button and enjoy.

Desert USA

www.desertusa.com/Thingstodo/du_ttd_treasure.html

Very comprehensive for the western United States.

High Desert Insider

www.highdesertinsider.com/html/rockhunting.html

Excellent for Southern California.

Eclectic Arcania Blog

http://eclecticarcania.blogspot.com/2012/03/mojave-desert-mini-rockhounding.html

Excellent for the Mohave Desert.

Hi-Desert Rockhounds
www.hi-desertrockhounds.org
> Very active crew.

Legends of America
www.legendsofamerica.com/trs-desertrockhounding.html
> Information about ghost towns.

Utah.com
www.utah.com/hike/rock_hounding.htm
> Great for Utah.

Wind River, Wyoming
www.windriver.org/do.php?cat=attractions&keyword=Rock%20Hounding
> Great for Southwest Wyoming.

Barstow BLM
www.blm.gov/ca/st/en/fo/barstow/rock.html
> BLM's Barstow, California, office.

Rockhound Trips
http://rockhound.tumblr.com
> Wide-ranging field trips.

Remember to treat the desert with respect and tread lightly. Avoid the temptation to kill wildlife for trophies. If you shoot a gun, police your brass. If you bring beverages in a bottle or a can (cans are better), collect your empties and carry them back to civilization. Bring a plastic bucket to pack up extra trash that you might find. Any trash seen around a

Please use common sense when confronting wildlife. Those rattles are even more valuable to the snake.

popular rockhounding locale will be attributed to rockhounds, so do everything you can to make sure we don't get a bad reputation.

TAILINGS

The tailings piles at abandoned mines often have interesting material, but not always. You may be in an area where the commodity in question was disseminated gold invisible to the naked eye, bound up in limestone, rhyolite, or altered ash beds. In many cases, however, miners tossed aside piles and piles of crystallized quartz, crystallized calcite, pyrite, and other lesser sulfides. Copper mines in the Seven Devils region of Idaho, for example, are frequently littered with rocks rich in green malachite. Abandoned mines are often a great place to search for minerals, but always be cautious about shifting boulders. Avoid dangerous overhanging cliffs, and stay out of underground workings unless you are an experienced spelunker assisted by a competent crew.

For example, in Washington State a group known as Northwest Underground Explorations (www.nwuemines.com) has done a superb job of researching, investigating, and documenting underground mines throughout the state. They use hard hats, safety ropes, and lots of common sense. They offer a series of outstanding books about the various mining districts they have inspected, and their write-ups often include sections entitled "For the rockhound," where they describe what they found in the tailings. Many similar groups exist throughout the United States, so if you want to venture underground, search one out.

Be sure to use common sense around old mining structures like the one found near Wallace, Idaho, shown in the photo. Buildings that date to the late 1880s are just looking for an excuse to come down. They are firetraps and often host colonies of rats and mice that could spread the hantavirus.

Old mining structures are best appreciated with a camera. Stay out unless you have permission, have all the necessary gear, and hook up with a safety-minded club!

Old openings and mine shafts are even more dangerous than old buildings. Stick to the tailings piles out in the clean, fresh air.

There are two types of rockhounds: those who look at a hole in the ground and see danger and those who see opportunity. If you are the former, move on and stay in the light. If you are the latter, that's fine—but you need to have the right gear to go down that hole. You need experience, a support team, gear, training, and some kind of plan or knowledge of what's below.

Ghost Towns
Part of the charm of rockhounding around old mines and tailings piles is in learning the stories of the old ghost towns. Here are some links to help in that regard.

Ripley's
www.ripleysghosttowns.com/listings.html
 Some interesting ghost stories.

Ghost Town Explorers
www.ghosttownexplorers.org
 Great stuff; nice links, too.

High Desert Drifter
http://highdesertdrifter.com
   One of the best sources of information on ghost towns in the American West.

Ghost Towns USA
www.ghosttowns.com/ghosttownsusa.html
   Crowd-sourced; plenty of photos.

Legends of America
www.legendsofamerica.com/ghosttowns.html
   Lots of history.

Southern Cal fun places
www.socalfunplaces.com/topic_desert.htm
   Good link to the Hauser geode beds.

Basically, rockhounding at abandoned mines and tailings piles requires much more diligence and safety awareness, but the rewards can be bigger too.

VEINS AND VUGS

Chiseling material from a rock outcrop is hard work involving heavy hammers and a lot of safety equipment. You need to protect your eyes with goggles, protect your head with a hard hat, and protect your hands and knuckles with sturdy gloves. Not everyone is willing to do all that work, as Cora B. Houghtaling noted in her 1967 book, *Rockhounding Out of Bishop:*

> Not being much of a digger myself, I tire of one spot and
> would rather roam. Up a sand wash or around a rocky ledge, I
> am always sure that soon I'll stumble onto the proverbial 'gold
> mine' and, strange as it might seem, sometimes I do. (p. 18)

Still, others enjoy using heavy tools to liberate prizes from a ledge or cliff they tracked down.

Rockhound club attacking a rhodonite vein at Mount Higgins, Washington

Electric Jackhammer

If you are lucky enough to find a good outcrop that is also near a road, you might consider bringing a portable generator and an electric jackhammer, such as shown in the accompanying graphic. Here's a link to a new Bosch "Brute" that can do the trick: www.youtube.com/watch?v=2Oyl4A561po.

Another site to check is Grainger (www.grainger.com). Harbor Freight (www.harborfreight.com) could also hook you up.

Paleontologist ReBecca Hunt-Foster ("DinoChick") demonstrates how to be productive with an electric jackhammer.

Dynamite Crystal Collector

Bob Jackson has recovered numerous quartz crystal plates from his famed Spruce Ridge crystal quartz claim at Snoqualmie Pass, Washington, and from his fluorite claim at Rock Candy Mine in British Columbia. He even hosted Cash and Treasures *star Kirsten Gum there for an episode.*

My undergraduate degree is in hydrology. Other than occasional work pointing out that water flows downhill, I haven't pursued that career. I did graduate studies in mineralogy, and through a rather convoluted path, minerals became my destiny.

My typical workday now is very similar to a construction worker. My crew and I drill, blast, and then clear away the blast rubble looking for crystal specimens. Crystals are fragile and very sensitive to shock. A tiny amount of damage can reduce the value of a specimen by 90 percent. My proprietary blasting method put me in demand for mining valuable, delicate things.

Other positive developments for mineral collectors are the diamond chainsaw, allowing most anything to be cut out of solid rock, and hydrofracturing—cutting rock with high-pressure water.

FOSSIL COLLECTING

Use this section to familiarize yourself with the different aspects of fossil collecting. Note that when done properly, collecting fossils is probably the most purely scientific activity in this handbook. There is still a lot of work to do in piecing together the fossil record, and it's always possible that your discovery could be significant. You need to pay attention to detail in order to make sure your collecting locale gets recorded properly. Also, becoming a competent fossil collector requires excellent knowledge of biology, physiology, and related fields. Depending on where your interests take you, you may need to be able to identify the insides of flowers, the small bones of tiny mammals, or evidence of hair or feathers.

An excellent starting resource is the *Fossil Collector's Handbook*, written by Gerhard Lichter and translated into English. He covers finding, identifying, preparing, and displaying fossils; and while he mostly covers European collecting locales, his information is timeless and complete.

Use Table 5 to give yourself an idea of what to expect or what might be a significant find for a particular time period. For example, if it was your lifetime ambition to discover the North American equivalent of Lucy (*Australopithecus afarensis*), an extinct hominid that lived between 3.9 and 2.9 million years ago and is shown in the accompanying image, you'd know to restrict your search to Pliocene sedimentary rocks.

The "Holy Grail" for North American fossil hunters would be to find the equivalent of the skull of "Lucy," an early primate. This reproduction is from www .valleyanatomical.com.

Table 5: Geologic Time and the Fossil Record

Era	Period	Time (in millions)	Significant Fossils
Cenozoic	Holocene	Now–11,000 years ago	Modern life
	Pleistocene	0.011–1.8	Homo sapiens
	Pliocene	2–5	Australopithecines
	Miocene	5–26	Hominids
	Oligocene	26–38	Grasses, anthropoids
	Eocene	38–54	Big land mammals
	Paleocene	54–65	Mammals diversify
Mesozoic	Cretaceous	65–136	Primates emerge
	Jurassic	136–190	Flying reptiles
	Triassic	190–225	Dinosaurs, mammals
Paleozoic	Permian	225–280	Reptiles
	Pennsylvanian	280–325	Coal swamps; conifers
	Mississippian	325–345	Seed ferns
	Devonian	345–395	Sharks, spiders, amphibians
	Silurian	395–430	Land plants, jawed fishes
	Ordovician	430–500	Gastropods, vertebrates
	Cambrian	500–570	Trilobites, graptolites
Precambrian Super Eon (eons and eras left off)		570–700	Jellyfish, arthropods
		700–1,000	Sponges
		1,000–1,400	First advanced cells
		1,400–2,000	Primitive cells diversify
		2,000–3,000	First stromatolites
		3,000–3,400	First primitive cells
		4,600	Our solar system formed

Legal Notice

Collecting vertebrate fossils is illegal on public lands without a paleontological permit. Violators will be prosecuted under the "theft of government property" provision of 18 United States Code (USC), section 641, and may face a minimum fine of $1,000 and a year in jail, up to $10,000 and ten years in jail. Permits to paleontologists are available from BLM state offices.

However, such offices rarely issue permits to amateurs. If you truly want to grow up to be a dinosaur hunter, your best bet is to go to school, get a degree, and affiliate yourself with a museum, university, or other research organization that can easily pull permits.

Sir David Attenborough recently acknowledged that given the strict new laws on the books in Great Britain, he would not likely be a fossil hunter today. Here's a quote from the *Telegraph*, dated November 6, 2012, available at this link: www.telegraph.co.uk/earth/wildlife/9657545/David-Attenborough-I-would-never-have-been-a-naturalist-under-todays-fossil-laws.html.

Britain is losing generations of young naturalists because of laws banning children from collecting birds' eggs and fossils, according to Sir David Attenborough. The broadcaster said he would never have been able to pursue his interest in wildlife if current legislation had been in place when he was a boy. The Wildlife and Countryside Act of 1981 prohibits the removal of eggs from the nest of any wild bird, while being found in possession of a dead wild bird—or any part of one—is also an offence. Fossil–collecting is banned at Sites of Special Scientific Interest and is covered by numerous other guidelines. Speaking to Radio Times, Sir David, 86, said few children now ventured out to explore the natural world. He agreed that the situation was "a disaster in waiting."

In the book *Cruisin' the Fossil Freeway* by paleontologist Dr. Kirk Johnson and artist Ray Troll, Dr. Johnson argues that you are much better off sticking to invertebrates in your fossil collecting adventures for the legal reasons cited above.

Fossil hunters are especially interested in the concept of geological time. Gem collectors may be casually interested in the age of a granite intrusion that contains pegmatite dikes, but fossil hunters key in on specific time periods. The Geological Society of America has a handy PDF that shows the different time periods that make up Earth history at www.geosociety.org/science/timescale/timescl.pdf.

Fossil-collecting Links

Use the links below to get started mining the Internet for general fossil-collecting information.

Wikibooks

http://en.wikibooks.org/wiki/Fossil_Collecting
  Book-length; great resource.

Pocket Ranger

http://pocketranger.wordpress.com/2012/11/08/school-of-rocks-fossil
-collecting-for-beginners/
  Strictly for beginners.

Fossil Facts

www.fossils-facts-and-finds.com/fossil_collecting.html
  Good introductory information.

Texas Road Runners

www.txroadrunners.com/rockhoundpages/TexasRockHuntingSites/
TexasRockAndFossilSites.htm
  Mostly covers Texas, but a great site if you travel through that state.

Leaves

Fossil leaves are a great place to start a collection. Leaves are easy to understand and usually closely resemble a living plant. Because fossil leaves usually have living relatives, even a young collector can start to make assumptions about the environment that must have existed when the leaf was alive.

Fee Digging for Leaves

Here is a short list of fee-dig operations that cater to fossil leaf diggers.

Fossil Bowl

http://suite101.com/article/clarkia-idaho-fossil-bowl-a58492
http://en.wikipedia.org/wiki/Clarkia_fossil_beds
  Fee-dig spot for collecting Miocene leaves in Clarkia, Idaho; doubles as a motocross track.

Stonerose Interpretive Center and Eocene Fossil Site

www.stonerosefossil.org

Great spot for Eocene-age plant fossils, with occasional insects as well.

Paleobotanists have pieced together many clues about past climates by noting the collection of plant fossils they find. Perhaps

Leaf fossil from Fossil Bowl at Clarkia, Idaho

the clue to solving greenhouse gas emissions lies in studying plant life from the Permian. There is still much important work to do in this field.

Shells

One of the most vexing scientific questions for early philosophers was explaining how marine fossils ended up on top of the highest peaks. In his short, delightful book, *The Seashell on the Mountaintop*, Alan Cutler described the many theories of how fossil seashells came to be in solid rock. Ancient philosophers theorized spontaneous generation and nighttime precipitation and even blamed evil fairies. Cutler's book showed how Nicholas Steno reached the correct explanation.

Like fossil leaves, fossil shells are legal to collect, and the Internet is full of information to help you get started. This is an easy search on the Internet; at the search bar enter "fossil <type> <state>" and you should be rewarded with plenty of information to sift through. The following list provides an example of various links to videos, reports, and personal blogs.

Florida corals, limestones
www.dep.state.fl.us/geology/geologictopics/fossil-collecting.htm

Ohio Brachiopods
www.youtube.com/watch?v=8l8d7YzNz4I

Ohio marine organisms
www.dnr.state.oh.us/Portals/0/publications/pdfs/huestonwoodsfossils.pdf

Kansas corals
www.kgs.ku.edu/Extension/fossils/coral.html

New Mexico corals
http://scottgregory.info/fossils/paleo.article.016op.pdf

Arizona corals, bryozoans
www.safossils.com/idlinks.html

California sand dollars
www.youtube.com/watch?v=VRDg_DsHHeQ

General corals
http://geology.er.usgs.gov/paleo/corals.shtml

General large seashells
www.ehow.com/list_5745194_large-fossilized-sea-shell-identification
.html

Concretions

Concretions are both a blessing and a curse. On the plus side, they protect material from harm by wrapping up delicate fossils in a lime-rich,
solid casing. On the negative side, those casings are very hard to crack.

Concretions form in lime-rich mud when something—a rock, a claw,
a stick, or a 6-foot-long whale skull—begins to attract mud. Constant
agitation in the surf rolls the muddy material around and around, and
eventually a natural ball results.

Small concretions, jokingly called "caveman marbles," sometimes contain tiny fossils. This one contains an eroding crab claw.

This whale skull from near Coos Bay, Oregon, is wrapped in plaster around its concretion casing.

Not all concretions carry anything of interest. But that's part of the charm. Even the small, round concretions, sometimes called "caveman marbles," may contain a crab claw or a well-preserved snail.

As noted earlier, larger concretions can hold something really special. The concretion shown in the accompanying figure is a whale skull from the Oregon coast. Affectionately known as "Wally," it's still undergoing preparation by its discoverers at the North American Research Group (www.narg-online.com).

Bones

In her epic book *The First Fossil Hunters,* Adrienne Mayor managed to match discoveries of large fossil bones in the ancient world with some of the earliest myths and stories. For example, she noted the similarities between a protoceratops, the ancestor of the more common triceratops, and the mythological griffin that guarded gold. She found that the bones and skulls of protoceratops were numerous in an area of Mongolia that also contained valuable placer gold resources. She noted the rich fossil record of Pleistocene mammoths around the Mediterranean Sea and

Paleontology Pro

ReBecca Hunt-Foster is the new district paleontologist for the Bureau of Land Management, Canyon Country District, in Moab, Utah. She is the author of the Dinochick blogs at http://paleochick.blogspot.com.

I use to collect brachiopods, bryozoans, and crinoids that I would find back home in Arkansas. I enjoy collecting Cambrian trilobites with my husband and in the Oligocene badlands of a friend's private ranch in Nebraska.

I love the idea of working with rocks and fossils all day, and I enjoy having an excuse to explore and hike for work. I was really drawn to the kind of job where I would be outside working most of the time, but inside when it was really cold. I knew from the age of 13 that paleontology was what I wanted to do for the rest of my life.

PHOTO COURTESY OF REBECCA HUNT-FOSTER

showed how the pelvis of a large animal could also look like the eye sockets and skull of a giant race of humans.

Ever since those times, scientists, geologists, and paleontologists have struggled to figure out how such bones got where they are and what they represent. The first true dinosaur fossil was not recognized until the 1820s, but by the 1870s two American titans were driving teams of excavators across the western United States in search of large, intact skeletons. Edward Drinker Cope and Othniel C. Marsh started as friends but ended up bitter enemies devoted to ruining each other and naming species before the other guy could.

Two books cover these bone wars: *The Great Dinosaur Hunters and Their Discoveries* by Edwin H. Colbert and *The Bonehunters' Revenge: Dinosaurs and Fate in the Gilded Age* by David Rains Wallace. You'll get a true sense for just how competitive fossil collecting can get.

Many US museums have outstanding dinosaur skeletons on display. If you ever find yourself on a trip to Yellowstone National Park in Wyoming, consider a slight detour to Thermopolis, Wyoming, to take in the Wyoming Dinosaur Center. As shown in the accompanying figure, the curators there have done a marvelous job of staging their displays. Thermopolis also boasts some world-class hot springs and nearby Native American petroglyphs at Legend Rock.

Since excavating vertebrate fossils from public land is illegal without the right permits, your best bet for experiencing a dinosaur dig is

This Tyrannosaurus rex skull is on display at the Wyoming Dinosaur Center in Thermopolis.

to hook up with one of the many private digs. Refer to the list below for links to various options.

Paleo Adventures
www.paleoadventures.com/id4.html
>Dig sites in Wyoming, Montana, and South Dakota.

Prehistoric Store
www.prehistoricstore.com/item.php?item=852
>Dig sites in North Dakota, South Dakota, Wyoming, Montana, and Nebraska.

Baisch's Digs
www.dailydinosaurdigs.com
>Dig site in Montana.

DinoBlog
www.childrensmuseum.org/themuseum/dinosphere/dino_digs.htm
>Dig site in South Dakota.

Dinosaurs Rock
www.dinosaursrock.com/Utah_Fossil_Dig.html
>Dig site in Utah.

Dino Ridge
www.dinoridge.org/tours.html
>Dig site in Colorado.

Whatever type of fossil you want to collect, there is a lot of territory to cover. Use the Internet to your full advantage, and see if you can add your name to science.

GOLD PROSPECTING

Even rockhounds need to be able to pan material as they search for indicator minerals. However, the true experts at panning material are gold prospectors, with their modern, high-tech pans. A good pan full of rich pay dirt may even lead to a huge dredging operation such as shown in the figure here.

Star attraction at Sumpter Dredge State Park in eastern Oregon

Gold Prospectors Association of America
www.goldprospectors.org

All beginning gold prospectors should pay to be in at least one club, and the most obvious one is the Gold Prospectors Association of America (GPAA). For one thing, you can quickly get online and start taking advantage of the GPAA forums. It is easy to sign up, and there are thousands of posts covering hundreds of topics. You will find information ranging from trip reports, gold district history, current regulations, and comments about the latest version of the *Mining Guide.* It is a great way to maximize your membership value, because you can interact with some of the most perceptive prospectors around.

How to Use a Gold Pan

The key to successful gold prospecting is to increase your odds by concentrating a lot of material down to a very rich sample. You do not need expensive tools to bring home black sands each time out; you just need a gold pan and the ability to put out some effort. The more effort you expend, and the better your tools, the higher your odds of bringing home color every time—as long as you are in the right spots. That's why we covered research at the beginning of this book.

Basically, if you want better luck each time you head out to a gold-rich creek, you need to learn how to make a pile of "concentrates"—those black sands at the bottom of the pan. Do not even think of it as panning gold to start with, because there might not be any gold in your first few pans. Just think of this activity as *making concentrates.* If you can bring back half a cup or more of black sand each time you go out, it won't be long before you have enough "good stuff" to be of interest. If you save all your black sands and get out often enough, your goal may be as simple as a half-full five-gallon bucket weighing thirty pounds, which would be very interesting, indeed.

The best concentrates come from sluices and dredges, where you are cleaning up the rich residue from a ton or more of pay dirt that's been cleaned, sorted, and washed. But even a weekend gold panner can clean down a good pile of dirt into a bottle of concentrates. It depends on how much time and patience you have. Arm strength and good conditioning also help.

In fact, the nice thing about panning gold is that you do not need a lot of equipment. If you are traveling light, or just want to keep a Tupperware tub of essentials in your rig, you could go out to the gold country with just these few tools:

1. Gold pan

2. Hand trowel

3. Snuffer bottle

Your shovel would not even have to be very big; you could use a trowel. All you need is something to scoop material. If you want to start buying tools so that you can save energy, you can add a small screen to your equipment that sits on top of your gold pan and removes a lot of unnecessary big rocks. Then, once you pan down to a certain amount, usually about a tablespoon or less, you save it into a snuffer bottle (a small plastic bottle with a spout that you can use to suck up material in water, let settle, and squirt back out the water, preserving the black sands). Repeat ten or twenty times and you will be guaranteed to go home with some good material—if you chose a good spot.

The problem is that after you work through four or five pans, weighing ten or twenty pounds apiece, good old human ingenuity starts to kick in. A voice in your head starts to whisper, "There has to be a better way. . . ." And of course there always *is* a better way to mine gold. That's why there are catalogs and catalogs full of equipment to make your life easier, as well as row after row of vendors at gold shows. Just remember that you do not need those expensive machines until you've mastered the art of panning. And at the end of the day, those contraptions are just variations on, or combinations of, the screen, pan, and shovel. If you are a patient sort, and can take breaks so that you don't get too tired, you should be able to pan for six to eight hours in a good day. If you can pan ten pans per hour, you would get to almost a half a ton of material.

According to the 1918 *Mining Engineers Handbook,* written by Robert Peele, you could get about 267 cubic inches of material in a standard gold pan of his day. He thus calculated that 176 pans would equal one cubic yard of material, and that a reasonable goal would be to be able to move about 0.6 ton per day, or 105 pans.

Back in those days, real good pay dirt was worth about $10 per yard, so a miner could figure on making $6 a day in the California mother lode country. Figuring that the modern price of gold is about one hundred times the price back then, you can see that if there was just some good ground to work, even simple tools could build you a good poke.

There are two simple ways to get you closer to moving more than a half ton (1,000 pounds) of material per day. First, washing and screening out all the rocks and pebbles bigger than one-quarter inch in size will help enormously. Second, rather than spending the last five to ten minutes of each pan separating your finest material, you can just do a "check pan" every now and then, and set most of your concentrates aside for later.

Ordering Pay Dirt

Although the price of gold has made stocking bags of pay dirt such as shown in the figure on the next page a lot more expensive, you can still find many places willing to get you started. This is a quick, painless way to learn the techniques with enough color in the pan to make things worthwhile. Check out the links below to get started.

Felix's Pay Dirt
www.felixpaydirt.com

Gold Fever Prospecting
www.goldfeverprospecting.com

Eureka Joe's
www.eurekajoes.com

RR Paydirt
www.rrpaydirt.com

Got Nuggets
www.gotnuggets.com/paydirt.html

Bags of "salted" pay dirt are a great way to learn how to pan gold at home, before you venture into the field.

Steps for Panning Gold

Find a good spot to work, with a hole or quiet water area deep enough to let you sink your pan. Alternately, you can set yourself up with a big plastic tub and a hose to keep cleaning your dirty water. This has the advantage of taking pressure off your back and knees, and you should stay dry. Many older prospectors just bring back pay dirt in buckets to camp, set up a panning station on a picnic table, and save themselves a lot of strain. So your mileage may vary.

1. Fill your pan to about three-quarters or so with good material from a crack, crevice, behind a rock, under a rock, etc. Do not make it too heavy or you will wear yourself out quickly.

2. Suspend the pan in water and shake it around gently, mostly in a sloshing action, watching the material settle. Make it turn into a muddy liquid. Watch to see how much clay and mud starts to separate out. Do not let anything out of the pan except dirty water.

3. Check with your fingers to make sure you do not have any roots, twigs, lumps of clay, big rocks, or other problems. Break up the mud, moss, and clunks carefully. Let in more clean water and rinse your sample thoroughly several times, using your fingers to make sure your sample is breaking up. Remove any big rocks.

4. Keep shaking the pan, then swirling it gently, so that you can feel the lighter mud, clay, and other alluvium as they release. Keep rinsing, but do not do much more than pour out dirty water. Keep shaking the pan with both hands and swirling it gently. You are trying to get everything agitated and swirling in a liquid state so that gravity will pull the heaviest material to the bottom of the pan.

5. Using one hand, opposite your biggest riffles, start sliding the material away so that all the heaviest black sands, gold, and garnets end up jammed against the lowest riffle of the pan while lighter material goes over the lip. Switch your agitation method now to resemble the actions of a sluice box. Gently shake the pan so that a small amount of material slips over the lip of the pan.

6. Stop emptying the pan every so often, and slide everything back to the middle. You might see black sands sliding back down the riffles. Let in some fresh, clean water, and agitate the pan to liquefy the contents. You should see more of the mud and silt as you concentrate everything all over again in that first riffle, or at least as best you can. Now shake the pan, gently tilt it so that your first riffle has all the good stuff you can imagine, and repeat the action of a sluice and slide a little more material out over the lip of the pan.

7. Stop emptying again, and slide everything back down. Reintroduce fresh water; rewash your sample. Get your fingers in there, and see how liquefied it feels. Shake and slide the pan so that your first riffle does more of its magic. Pick the pan up again, and mimic the actions of a sluice so that more of the light material washes over the riffles while the heavies stay concentrated. Repeat constantly.

8. Watch for lines of black sand that start to form across the flat bottom of the pan as you get your sample further concentrated. Watch for black sands against the edges too. Try not to lose the good material at this stage. You should have a cup or so of material now. At this point you can put a metal "safety pan" down to make sure you don't lose anything inadvertently. If you are using a tub, this is particularly easy to do.

9. Keep washing, stratifying, and shaking. From time to time you can rock your sample from side to side, as you probably have all light material at the top; this speeds your reduction time. You can brush big pebbles out over the edge with your fingers too. Chances are good that you only have a few small pieces of gold, and they are most likely sitting right against that front riffle.

10. When you have a small enough sample, stop and re-stratify, introduce some clean water, and check what you have. Most of your lighter tan, brown, or reddish-yellow silt and mud should be gone now. You want to get down to where you can see how much black sand material you have.

11. It will take some practice to learn how to tilt your pan and fan it out at the same time to reveal the heaviest concentrates remaining in the sample. If you know all the heavies are against that first riffle, you can wash and tilt so that your heavies sweep across a small section of the pan bottom, and that is where you should see colors. You can gently wash this material in the same direction and push away the black sands while the gold stays put. You should now know how good your sample is. If you do not see any gold, get out a hand lens and look closer. *Do not throw away this material.*

12. There is a technique called the "Blueberry Bounce," where you can tap an edge of your pan and watch the gold and heavies bounce right to that side. However, this only works if you have gold in the pan!

You can keep panning now, or you can slurp all those concentrates up in a snuffer bottle and start making another batch.

Classify and Stratify

There are two geological terms you need to know to understand the basic physics, chemistry, and geology of what is happening when you pan material: classification and stratification. Let's look at each of them in turn.

Classify

To classify material simply means to screen it. When you look at a shovel full of gravel, dirt, and rocks, you know what a jumble of different-size material you have. It is completely unclassified—it's all mixed up. By sending that shovel load through a series of screens, you can end up with the finest material, which saves a lot of time as you begin panning.

Ideally you should have at least two screen sizes. In most gold areas today, you do not have to worry about nuggets until you reach bedrock. So in addition to your one-quarter-inch mesh to get rid of the big rocks, you can also use a mesh that goes down to one-thirty-second of an inch. A piece of gold that will not go through that mesh is a nice flake and will stand out like a beacon. If you are finding these, you will have to go back to a larger mesh. That is what is known as "a good problem to have."

Stratify

To stratify material is to settle it in water so that different layers form, with the heaviest material at the lowest point. If you have ever looked at the rocks in a large cliff, you have seen different layers on a large scale. The study of those layers is called stratigraphy, and to map those layers you must create a "stratigraphic column." But leaving that aside for the geology students, you need to know what is happening in your pan, sluice, wheel, or dredge.

Maybe you have heard all this before, but it doesn't hurt to review. Water has a weight of 1 gram per cubic centimeter, or a specific gravity of 1. Anything lighter than that—wood, paper, leaves, oil, and moss—will float. Anything heavier will sink. What's interesting is that the heavier material sinks farther. For example, gold has a weight of about 19 grams per cubic centimeter. Black sands like titanium, ilmenite, or magnetite weigh about 4 or 5 grams per cubic centimeter. What that means is that gold, being heaviest, sinks the furthest. That is good news to anyone using a "gravity trap" (a fancy term for a gold pan, sluice, etc.) If gold "floated" on top of black sand, you could not recover it.

Get to Bedrock

Remember, the closer you get to bedrock, the better you will do. There will be more black sands, more garnets, more platinum and rare earth elements, and more metallic trash. If you find you are in excellent material and pulling out "picker-size" pieces of gold, you may want to adjust your operation and save whatever you are screening out into a bucket that you can search with a metal detector. You may want to stop screening and set up a dredge or high banker. You may start panning with a safety pan underneath just to make sure you do not lose anything in the final 10 percent of your pan. Alternatively, you may want to go to a closed system like a big tub of water so that any slip of the wrist or casual mistake can't cost you. All of these are good problems to have.

If you are in an area that has been worked over pretty hard, you need to have a good plan. Start a hole, and use a screen to get rid of half the volume before you even start swirling your pan. Save all your black sands, but only pan the material far enough down to see what you've got, without spending time to clean it up thoroughly.

- Time yourself, and see how fast you can get a pan down to concentrates. Time how long you can go before you need a rest.
- Use a safety pan and pan through it often to make sure you are not getting tired or careless.
- Use smaller Tupperware bowls if you don't want to use a five-gallon bucket.
- Make yourself a handy panning kit that fits into a container so that you can pack fast.
- Bring a hand lens to look over those black sands. Check for garnets, quartz, etc.
- Bring at least one, and preferably more, snuffer bottles for slurping up material.
- Consider a plastic bottle with a lid you can dump your snuffer bottle into.
- Bring vinegar to burnish off the tarnish of gold/silver electrum.

For a detailed view of how one miner worked locales on the Clearwater River in Idaho, check out http://bedrockorbust.blogspot.com. The adventures of "Bedrock Bob" are a joy to read.

Choosing the Right Gold Pan

Any experienced gold prospector will tell you that the most important tool among all your gold mining equipment is the humble gold pan. Whether you are testing a creek, digging out dirt from a crevice, or cleaning up concentrates, there is no better companion.

But, like candy, it is hard to stop after just one pan. Even casual prospectors like to bring a stack of four or five pans with them when they go out, just in case. You might find you are more comfortable bringing a bigger pan for rough work and some smaller pans to finish concentrates. The truth is that there are many different pans out there, and they all have their strengths and weaknesses. In this section we will look at a wide variety of pans and give you the information you need to build a nice collection of your own.

Old Reliable

First, every gold panner needs a metal pan. The pan shown here is at least thirty years old, and it is still in good shape. It mostly gets used as a safety pan because it's not so prone to floating away, but it has seen service in a variety of camp duties as well. It has put in time as a giant ashtray and also to light charcoal. Metal pans can act as a large trowel to scoop dirt, clear holes, and dig ditches, although you will probably have to bend it back

This "old reliable" 11-inch metal pan works great as a "safety pan."

into shape afterwards. Some old-timers were known to admit they had been reduced to using a metal pan to boil water and fry eggs when they found they were without the usual pots and pans.

The truth is, you will not use the metal pan very often to just a plain pan. It makes a beautiful noise when it has gold nuggets rolling around; even the usual assortment of ball bearings, fishing weights, or other metal sliding across the bottom sound nice. But the lack of riffles is a nonstarter for most modern gold panners. Some newer metal pans have riffles, although they are more like bumps. Even with that, metal pans are heavy. The bottom line: The buildup of rust and dents just cannot compete with high-tech, purposefully engineered riffles, so let's move on.

Big Pans

The big 16-inch blue pan, shown in the photo on the next page, has even more going for it. It is lightweight for its size, and the bottom is nearly 9 inches across. That allows for a nice fanning action as you spread the final concentrates. The blue color is excellent for revealing gold and garnets, which is a big advantage over black pans that can have issues when playing with a lot of black sand. This particular pan has some real engineering going on with the riffles, which start out very aggressive, sporting a clever, sunken trap area. The second riffle also has serious bite, but the third and fourth riffles are not nearly as intense. They do have a sharp angle, so gold will trap against them while black sand is washing over the edge. Overall, the riffles are excellent. It is hard to pan something this big with one hand, but when you get the material going, you can feel those riffles biting, which gives you the confidence to get aggressive and really work it.

Big 16-inch blue pan

Close-up of riffles and trap area

The trap area shown in the bottom photo also makes using a snuffer bottle easier.

The GPAA Classic

The 14-inch green GPAA pan shown on the next page is included in the membership packet when you join their club, and it is a favorite for many regular gold panners. It is the standard Garrett gravity-trap style and has been around for a long, long time. The 14-inch size is easier to use with one hand, but it still holds plenty of material. There are four riffles, each with a sharp, aggressive bite, allowing for respectable work with heavy black sands. You can stop using the riffles when you get down to a couple tablespoons of material and rotate over to the smooth side. Or you can transfer the whole load to a finishing pan or snuffer bottle and start a new batch.

The bottom is wide, almost 8 inches, which gives you a good view of your material when you look for that flash in the pan.

You will see some interesting variations on this simple design. The number of riffles can go up to six, which you will appreciate in areas with heavy black sands.

Classic 14-inch green GPAA pan

12-inch Pans—Not Just for Kids

After panning for great lengths of time, as the day goes on you may find yourself eventually switching to smaller pans just to save your arms and shoulders. The 12-inch pan shown in the photo comes in handy when you are getting worn out, but it is also great for kids, grandparents, and moms because it is easier to handle. There are usually only three riffles, with decent bite to them, and the bottom is around 6 inches in diameter. Make sure you check the riffles and don't find much round-ing—you want a good, sharp bite that will trap gold efficiently. You cannot process as much volume as you would with a bigger pan, but you might be able to work longer, and not fall asleep 5 minutes after dinner.

A standard 12-inch black pan with three riffles is great for anybody without a lot of arm strength.

A new favorite for many panners is the blue 12-inch, six-riffle design from Keene, with an almost 8-inch bottom, as shown in the photo on the next page. The riffles are sharp and trap gold easily, giving you confidence that you can work fast. When you get material down far enough, there are twenty micro-riffles that really let you work through black sands. Thanks to the blue color, large gold pieces show up immediately.

This 12-inch blue pan from Keene has two sets of riffles.

Micro-riffles on the left and regular riffles on the right give you two different panning actions.

Finishing Pans

When you have material that is screened, sorted, and concentrated, you do not need the big pans any more—you need a smaller pan for maximum control. If you like a deeper pan with a small bottom, try the small green 10-inch pan with four riffles and a 3-inch bottom for finishing work, as shown in the photo. It has a nice, light feel, and you should be comfortable with it for long stretches of time. Or you might find that the small bottom is just not right for your needs. This pan comes in particularly handy when you're setting up a smaller panning tub with a metal safety pan, for example, and will even work in a standard cooler filled with water instead of iced beverages.

Another new favorite is the small blue Keene pan shown to the right. It has five regular riffles and

Small green finishing pan with very limited bottom

This small blue 10-inch finishing pan from Keene has a wide bottom and two sets of sharp riffles.

fifteen micro-riffles, and the bottom is almost 6 inches across. It works extremely well for concentrates by virtue of the dual riffles, and the wide blue bottom is handy for your fanning action.

Hex Pan

Available through Black Cat Mining (www.blackcatmining.com/mining-equipment/hex-pan.cfm), the Hex pan is 14 inches wide, with a nice, broad bottom, two sets of aggressive riffles, and one set of fine riffles, as shown in the photo. Don't be put off by its funny shape. You probably do more dipping to

The 14-inch Hex Pan has a good assortment of aggressive riffles.

allow the material in your pan to run across riffles than you do circulating the material. So having six flat sides makes a lot of sense.

Copper Pans

Since you will not normally work with mercury, you may not have the urge to get a nice copper pan. By far their most common use historically was with mercury, which few miners bother with anymore. The likely use for a copper pan today is as a decorative item, from a small, 4-inch copper pan all the

Copper pans are mostly decorative, although the smaller pan is handy for setting aside nice specimens.

way up to 12- and 16-inch varieties. These pans do not get out to the field much, but if they do, they develop an attractive patina very quickly.

Bateas

If you are curious about what other cultures use to pan gold, run a search for the term *batea.* It is a conical, 2-foot wooden bowl with a sharp, pointed middle about 6 inches or so in depth. All heavy material is trapped in the conical middle, but you'd think it would be overwhelmed quickly by black sands or other heavies. If you've seen the History Channel series *Bamazon,* you have seen one in action. Wooden bateas get waterlogged quickly, but a metal or high-tech plastic version might work well.

Whatever your next pan is, chances are good it will be the right one. And remember: The problem is not too much black sand; the problem is not enough gold.

Panning Machines

If you have been panning gold for a season or two, you are most likely bringing home a lot of black sand and a little gold each time you go out. If you are getting good enough that the concentrates are piling up, you are probably ready to take the next step: purchasing some kind of panning machine to help separate the gold.

If you are a good, patient gold panner and are into an area with decent gold, you can pan and pan until you separate the gold yourself. The problem comes when you pan out some gold from a sample with heavy black sand, re-pan your tailings to make sure you are getting it all, and find a bunch of gold in your tailings. Now you know the black sands are interfering with your stratification. A machine of some sort is a pretty good investment if you have that problem a lot.

In this section we will look at some of the leading gold panning machines on the market and explore what they do. We will talk about their strengths and, as you read the information, try to figure out what type of mechanical help you need. Some machines are good at working through raw pay dirt, making rich concentrates that are full of gold and black sands. Other machines can completely clean your gold from the accompanying material. Finally, some machines have settings that allow you to perform both tasks.

At present, state fish and game departments in the West do not regulate these kinds of machines, so you don't have to apply for permits. However, as soon as this book hits the shelves, some new law may take effect, or some warden could interpret laws already on the books in a certain way. You may want to compare notes from this book with advice from other longtime prospectors. If you go on an outing, you can probably watch all these machines in action and form an even better opinion.

No machine accomplishes all tasks with perfection. In order to narrow your search, you have to figure out what you need the machine to do. What are your needs? Do you have a five-gallon bucket full of concentrates that you want to clean out? Or do you clean material up as you go? Have you been crevicing and cleaning mossy boulders for most of your weekend trips and just want to save your shoulders from a lot of panning? Keep your answers to questions like these in mind as we go along.

The three different machines we will look at are as follows:

1. Gold Magic, a spiral panning machine that does not require a pump

2. Desert Fox, a spiral panning machine that uses a small, aquarium-style water pump

3. Power Sluice, a miniature high-banker and sluice arrangement that also uses a pump

There are other pieces of equipment out there, but you will find these three types represent most of the machines you can buy.

Gold Magic Spiral Pan

www.goldmagic.com

The Gold Magic spiral pan works in a tub or in the creek.

Century Mining Equipment offers a panning machine with great flexibility. It is fine for final cleanup if you adjust the angle properly and is easy to use either in a tub or out in running water.

There are some ingenious aspects to the design that you should know about; for example, you can purchase a stripped-down unit that works on a hand crank rather than a motor.

First off, the Gold Magic shown in the figure does not have to sit in its own tub to be effective. This machine can operate in a creekbed, after you carve out a little depression for it to stand in. The important thing is to get the water line right across the middle of the pan and to get the angle right. The more severe the angle, the less black sand you will capture in the cup in the middle.

Second, the Gold Magic has a set of clever bumps along the outside spirals, which serve to break up the sand and soil going through the machine. These bumps help the Gold Magic also work as a dry washer system, inserting air into the mix so that gravity can do its work even in dusty pay dirt. The Gold Magic is the only machine in this category that works wet or dry.

Third, the machine does not rely on a pump, which means you do not have to worry about the water staying clean. This is a big advantage, as the pump is often the weakest link in a gold-panning machine. If you are working with clay or silt, the pump's intake can clog, even with a nylon stocking around the intake. Having said that, however, it is still best to work with the cleanest water possible.

The tricky part of operating the Gold Magic spiral pan is getting the angle of the unit just right. Also, it's pretty easy to lose the little container that fits in the middle, but you can use a small suction bottle to clean it out, so that's not a big deal. Probably the most fascinating part is using the suction bottle to slurp up that small eddy of floating gold. It turns out that very small gold particles will attach to any grease in the water, and you can often see a little "raft" of oils, dirt, and microscopic gold swirling in an eddy.

The Gold Magic has many accessories, including a solar panel capable of either charging the battery or running the machine.

Desert Fox Gold Panning Machine
www.desfox.com

Camel Mining Products offers a great device for relieving your panning chores. It is incredibly efficient when you adjust the water flow from the arm properly. It sets up fast, operates in its own tub, and goes through material quickly.

The Desert Fox shown in the photo is a compact system that comes in a rugged little carrying case. The unit takes up the least amount of space in the truck and is simple and logical to set up. Still,

The Desert Fox spiral pan is great for cleaning black sands.

you will probably find that the adjustments for the Desert Fox are the trickiest to get right, and it takes a little trial and error to figure them out. On the other hand, this is the best machine for getting to clean gold, and only clean gold, in the final cup.

There are several competing products on the market, but this one has been around a long time—according to the company, at least forty years.

The Desert Fox also operates on a twelve-volt battery, which runs a small aquarium pump and spins the spiral pan. The water circulates through the system and out along a copper tubing arm, which provides several small jets of water to wash the riffles as material moves toward the center of the spirals. Gold tends to stay put, while the lighter material is washed down. Finally, the gold passes to the center of the pan and then through a hole to a small cup that dangles from a hook behind the unit. One common mistake is to forget to remount the small bucket after cleaning it out. This requires you to clean out the tub the machine sits in, which can be aggravating.

The Desert Fox spiral pan is a premier concentrate cleaner; that is the number-one job for this little powerhouse. The unit has a good "appetite" for material, and you can experiment how fast you can push it. The website says the machines can clean seventy pounds of pay dirt per hour.

Micro-Sluice

Micro-Sluice Gold Products (www .micro-sluice.com) offers a variety of units that come in handy for final cleanup or actual sluicing, depending on whether you use the carpeting or the ribbed plastic. The general name for these devices is a "power sluice."

The small Gold Duster Power Sluice, shown in the photo, was created by Randy Wilson and was a staple at GPAA gold shows. It is representative of the whole category of power sluices.

The Power Sluice can process raw material or clean concentrates.

Micro-Sluice models run from a small, one-bucket "Micro-Sluice Junior" all the way up to a larger unit that you can set up along a creek. The systems are good for pulling gold out of black sand, but to reach peak efficiency, you want to set up in a controlled, laboratory-type environment where the system is closed.

The thing you will probably like most about these small sluices is that they have an exit for bigger material off the top rack. The system is not so rugged that you want to shovel big rocks at it, but you can clean material in the top hopper with ease. The grating is angled so that big material does not pass to the bottom.

In other words, these devices are great for *making* concentrates, which will save you a lot of panning time. You can use the heavy carpeting in the lower riffles and bypass the hand-panning step completely. The system is so easy to break down into a five-gallon bucket that you may never find you have run it "too long" just to see what happens. The carpeting cleans up fast, and you can quickly slosh water through the top and bottom sections.

Once you've cleaned up a few times, and are ready to see what you've got, you can switch out to the ribbed plastic matting, carefully push your concentrates through, and just collect gold. The key here is patience and time. If you are cleaning gold-rich concentrates that are dark and heavy with black sands, you cannot just dump the material in. You have to go slowly and let running water do its thing.

Blue Bowl

Keene Engineering also makes a Blue Bowl that works with a hose to push material around quickly and easily. You consume only three gallons of water per minute, and there are no parts to wear out other than the hose connection itself. At one of the top gold prospecting forums, http://au-prospecting.com/gold1/viewtopic.php?f=10&t=162, one contributor suggested making sure you clean your bowl to remove all the oils, then classify your material, and be very careful when regulating the water flow. He also suggested using sandpaper on the bowl, but you can read that for yourself.

Final Thoughts on Panning Machines

In the end, your mileage may vary, but which machine you purchase depends on what you need. If you already have a dredge, sluice, or high-banker, you probably just need to clean up concentrates; a Desert Fox is the way to go, because once you get it set, it is highly efficient. If you want a machine that works in the creek, at camp, and in the desert, go with the Gold Magic, as it hits a lot of sweet spots. If you want to clean up material straight from the crevice or moss bucket, without doing a lot of hand panning, the Micro-Sluice is a great machine.

Each of these units is compact, lightweight, and fairly quiet. Gas-powered engines are great for moving vast quantities of material, but they can leave your ears ringing and tend to intrude on the great outdoors. These small twelve-volt systems are much quieter and are super-efficient.

No matter which type you settle on, you will be glad you did. But be forewarned. Once you're processing your concentrates faster, you have a new problem: You need to make more concentrates!

Concentrate Cleanup

Here is a two-step concentrate cleanup system involving a magnetite remover and a small, green table. There are several varieties of magnetite removers, so you might get inspired to invent your own.

Magna-Two Magnetite Remover

The Magna-Two, formerly sold at www.goldcatcher.biz/the-magna-two .html and shown in the photo, works on dry material. For a test run, you could collect a sample of black sands from the beach, dry them out, and run them through. The material should be dark, heavy, and powdery.

This Magna-Two magnetite remover is sitting in a shallow plastic tub (not included).

If you've used common magnets to remove magnetite from gold concentrates, you know that you occasionally remove gold as well. The Magna-Two solves that by adding vibration to its magnetic system. You can see by the figure that the contraption is simple. It works on gravity and electricity and is easy to operate. Turn on the power source, comprising eight 1.5-volt batteries, and the action begins. Powerful magnets reach through the sheet aluminum, while the motor rattles the tray vigorously, vibrating away any nonmagnetic material.

Using the beach sand sample, several big, dark magnetite "blobs," or "islands," soon appear as black magnetite moves to the magnet, while the pay dirt pours off the end into a tub. In the figure you can see that the magnetite starts to grow spikes and tendrils when it's ready to dump. Once you

Small magnetite "islands" starting to build

have built up a lot of magnetite, you stick a small pan or plastic tray under the ramp, lift it from the magnets, and let the magnetite run off.

It doesn't take long to figure out how to sprinkle your concentrates lightly so that the magnets can work most efficiently. The device makes a pretty loud racket, but it works very well; you can rerun your material if you want to test it.

Gotcha Water Table

The Gotcha Water Table, available at http://gpex.ca/ads/gotcha.html and shown in the photo, works on gravity, with a water pump in a large tub that recirculates constantly. Once you set it up, following the easy instructions, you add a few drops of Jet-Dry automatic dishwasher conditioner, which serves to reduce the surface tension of the water. This ensures that your finest gold doesn't float away.

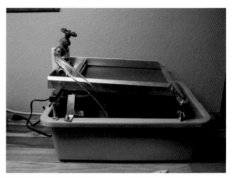

The Gotcha Water Table uses a thin sheet of water and gravity to wash away lighter material, leaving the gold behind.

A very thin sheet of water flows across the green table surface, fast enough to carry away light material but not so boisterous as to move the heavier gold. There are no riffles—the surface is plenty rough enough with its painted surface, full of micro pits and bumps, thanks to the familiar green chalkboard paint. This surface gives the ability to see even the tiniest gold colors.

By just sprinkling material onto the top of the table, you can control how fast the system works. The water flow pushes slowly but surely against the concentrates, and the lighter material flows quickly downward.

A YouTube video about the process (www.youtube.com/user/nuggetbill#p/a/u/1/16REqjjWGKw) helps a lot. (Search on "nuggetbill," and pull up his four videos.) You'll see how to use the included paintbrush to move material around; and because it's a closed system, you can't really lose anything.

By treating one area as "the gold zone" and moving material toward it carefully, you should accumulate a small pile of gold from your sample. See the accompanying figure on the next page.

This is an ideal setup for cleaning up your collection of concentrate samples from multiple trips. You can take a picture of each jar and then, once cleaned, you can take a picture of the result. If you remember about how much work went into producing each sample, you'll get a pretty good idea of where you might want to return.

Best of all, you can see from the glass vial photo that the result is very clean gold.

Carefully brush the clean gold to one side for easy pickup.

Clean gold extracted in a single afternoon from multiple samples

Advanced Cleanup

Todd Hoffman of Gold Rush: Alaska *has had some phenomenal cleanups on his Yukon gold claim.*

Our new cleanup procedure is pretty sweet. We fill up this 6-foot trough with water, just like you'd let horses drink from. We rinse the carpets off real well and get them clean. We shovel out the sluices and get all that material into the trough. It is all raw concentrates and weighs about 1,200 pounds. Then we shovel all that into a special duplex jig. It has a little shaker deck on top and splits the material. It had a long tom in the back too. We tested it and double-tested it to verify that it was clean coming out the end, but the bottom line was we took that 1,200 pounds down to thirty pounds of super-rich concentrates.

Next we screen that thirty pounds of material with a twenty-mesh screen. What we take off using the screen might fit into half a gold pan, but that pan is a sight for sore eyes, let me tell you. The remaining twenty-eight pounds is now ready for a shaker table, and it comes off in about two hours. So in about three hours, you've cleaned up for the week. Dad would dry it, weigh it, and report out the count at the campfire.

TODD HOFFMAN, *GOLD RUSH*, DISCOVERY CHANNEL

Final Thoughts on Recovery

Back in the earliest days of the GPAA television shows, founder George Massie used to tell a story about cleaning up his concentrates in an outside shack, where it was cold and drafty. He didn't mind too much, he said, and he'd take his time cleaning up buckets of gold-rich black sand with all kinds of contraptions. Still, he admitted, it would be better to be able to do his cleanup inside the warmth of his own house.

When he found a big bonanza hole on the Stanislaus River and recovered about 800 ounces of gold in one summer, he was finally allowed to do his cleanup in the front room. Which just goes to show—if you find enough good material, a lot of your problems will be solved.

Bigger Gold Mining Equipment

Once you've been out a few times and learned how to dig material from a crevice or from under big rocks, it's logical to move up in machine value and production capability. Refer to Table 6 for a look at the normal progression.

Sluices

Using a sluice box is a nice introduction to real gold mining. Some sluices, such as the E-Z Sluice (www.GoldFeverProspecting.com) shown in the figure, are very helpful for cleaning up concentrates in a tub or stream. When used in a stream, a sluice box almost always requires a heavy rock to keep it stable.

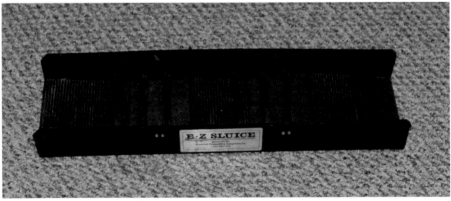

This short 24-inch E-Z Sluice is useful for starting out.

The Jobe fold-up sluice shown in the figures on the next page is available from Black Cat Mining (www.blackcatmining.com/mining

The Jobe fold-up sluice is perfect for backpacking to a secret location.

-equipment/folding-sluice.cfm). The sluice is 50 inches long when stretched out but only 15 inches long when folded up.

Folded up, the Jobe sluice is only 15 inches long.

The accompanying photograph shows a sluice box properly set up in a creek. While one miner accumulates pay dirt in buckets, the other can process material.

Simple sluice setup, with rocks adjusted in a wing-dam to help with flow

Table 6: Gold Mining Equipment Descriptions

Machinery	Description	Benefit	Drawback
Gold pan	Most common tool.	Inexpensive, quiet. Easy to set up.	Tiring, less-productive.
Rocker box	Two-story box setup to wash gravel without a pump.	Not very expensive. Quiet. Can move more gravel than a pan.	Not always highly efficient; need lots of water.
Sluice	Long trough with riffles and carpet set in creek.	Inexpensive, quiet. Moves plenty of pay dirt.	Difficult to get set up correctly without practice.
High-banker	Pumps water to raised sluice away from creek.	Efficient; good for teams of miners.	More costly; noisy. Water access can be an issue.
Dry washer	Uses air to mimic water; used in desert.	Best way to move lots of material in the desert.	Noisy, dusty, and not as efficient as using water.
Dredge	Pumps water to one or more sluices; for use in creek or river. Waste material dumps out at end of sluice.	Best way to reach bedrock in moving water. Suction hose is highly efficient.	Requires diving, more permits; only workable in limited season.
Trommel	Classic wash plant. Pumps water to round cylinder with holes; concentrates also move across sluice. Waste material piles up at end.	Washes gravel, removes waste, and then sluices remainder. Up to 97 percent efficient.	Expensive to buy and operate. Requires team of miners and heavy machinery.

Rocker Boxes

One of the earliest contraptions for washing gravel was the rocker box, a simple design that allowed one or two men to move a lot more material than a gold pan ever could. There are plans for simple rocker boxes on the Internet, and you see them at shows. Take a look at the clever new design in the figure.

The Rockin Gold Grabber, available at www.golddredge builders.com/rockin.html, takes that idea and advances it considerably. The hand-operated pump means no more dipping and pouring and can be recirculated. These devices are quiet, economical, and environmentally friendly—and they move a lot of pay dirt.

The Rockin Gold Grabber is a modern twist on an old idea.

High-bankers and Power-sluices

The term *high-banker* originally applied to a sluice box that was not attached to a dredge but still used pumped water to wash gravels. The idea was to be able to work high banks and benches, as long as you had a hose long enough to stretch to the water source. The term seems to be used less today, in favor of the term *power-sluice*, so be aware. Either way, you do not need a dredge permit, but many states still require paperwork; today there are numerous restrictions on working in stream banks

New CC690 Power Sluice from Advanced Mining Equipment (www.advancedmining equipment.com) in Long Beach, California PHOTO COURTESY OF JOSEPH CHMIEL

too. Still, since these devices do not rely on deep water and suction, you can set them up in the shade and bring up buckets of pay dirt to work through quickly and build nice concentrates with ease. The device seen in the photo is extremely efficient and will process a lot of material in a day if you have the right crew.

Dry-washers

For gold prospectors who operate in the desert, a dry-washer is a must. You can't bring enough water with you to operate a high-banker, so a dry-washer is the next best thing. Multiple videos on YouTube

demonstrate how to run a dry-washer. Check this one at www.youtube
.com/watch?v=ve9osr6QP-4.

Keen Engineering makes what they call the "King of the Dry-washers."
American Prospector Treasure Seeker sells them at www.aptsgold.com/
Keene151-drywasher.html.

Dredges

Dredges are efficient machines
that process a large amount of
material and reach far below the
water surface. A machine like
the one shown here, available
from D&K Detector Sales (www
.dk-nugget.com), would require
quite a bit of gold each day to pay
for itself. But on the right claim,
you would be happy after each
cleanup.

D&K Detector Sales in Portland, Oregon, manufactures
a complete line of sturdy, efficient dredges for creeks
or rivers.

Trommels

By the time you are considering a trommel, you are setting up a full
placer mining operation with permits and paperwork. You will need
excavators, earthmovers, bulldozers, and more. You will need pumps,
mechanics, operators, and you will need a full concentrate cleanup operation. Trommels are efficient and smart, and serious miners use some
form of trommel in their wash plant. You could start out with a small
trommel like the Goldzilla, shown in the photo, but eventually you'll
want to graduate to a larger setup like the Green Giant.

The Goldzilla gold trommel is small and portable.

The Green Giant is a 12-inch trommel
from California Sluice Box (www
.casluicebox.com).

PHOTO COURTESY OF DALE BABIN

Working in the Field **165**

Gold and Metal Detectors

Maybe you were one of those customers who had a blinking "12:00" on your VCR after a power outage before manufacturers learned to connect the clock to a battery. Maybe you have a teenage grand-daughter who does your computer maintenance because all that tech stuff makes you feel like you just got your knuckles rapped with a ruler. You may be an official "technophobe," with the plaque to prove it, but that does not mean you cannot enjoy metal detecting.

In this section we will identify many different areas on the Internet where you can study from the comfort of your own keyboard, away from prying eyes and youthful scorn. There is a ton of information out there, because "electronic prospectors" are a chatty and prolific group. For now, let's concentrate on "crowd-sourced" information from regular users; you can follow the manufacturer links as you get the vocabulary and concepts down.

First let's check in with Joseph Chmiel, an enthusiastic nugget hunter at www.advancedminingequipment.com/Nuggetshooting.html. He sells the Fisher Gold Bug Pro and strongly believes in it. He calls it "the single best value in a gold detector today! Fantastic sensitivity, superior discrimination and an affordable price. I have trained half a dozen people on this detector over the last few months and I am proud to say that every one of them has found gold. (No, not just their test nugget.) They all scored their very first nugget with this detector . . . even my 7-year-old son Jeffrey! He took my Pro, set it in the discriminate mode, and soon bagged his first 'wild' gold nugget! If you want bang for your buck, or just a great all around detector, this is it."

Known as "Lucky Joe," Chmiel has written articles, made YouTube videos (search for "LuckyJOE"), and even won Fisher's recent detecting video contest. If price were no object, he would steer you to the Minelab GP/GPX pulse induction detector. The Minelab finds the deeper, larger nuggets, even in terrain with numerous "hot rocks" that give out false readings. Says Joe: "My GPX4500 comes in handy in deep soil with hot rocks. Check out the pair of nuggets I found recently in the same hole" [shown in the figures on the next page]. "The big one was on top at 6 inches deep and the smaller one 4 inches farther down . . . my lucky day! I heard them first with an ear blast while using the 4500 but brought over the Gold Bug 2 for pinpointing. . . . It had no problem hearing the big one at that shallow depth either."

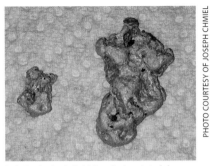

Left: Lucky Joe's Gold Bug 2 pinpointed these gold nuggets.
Right: "Lucky Joe" Chmiel found these two nuggets, weighing 17.09 and 2.1 grams, with a Minelab GPX4500 metal detector.

Joe says he uses the Gold Bug 2 more in the desert, where there is shallow bedrock. "A Fisher Gold Bug 2 VLF finds the tiniest of flakes near the surface. The Gold Bug Pro is also a contender in this department, with excellent sensitivity and superior discrimination capability. It can easily be used in a hot rock or iron-infested area and 'see' around the trash. I should also mention the price difference between Minelab and Fisher is about $5,000. You definitely get more bang for your buck with the VLF machines."

Jeff's Metal Detecting Site

http://jefferyvmckenzie.tripod.com/id4.html

Jeff McKenzie has packed his site with all kinds of personal information. After several fits and starts early in his career with cheaper units, he recently settled on a White's 5900 Di Pro. He returned to places where he got skunked with inferior technology and found himself pulling out coins, relics, and jewelry. He's been hooked ever since.

Jeff has four key points to consider when getting started, along with his overall premise, which is to have fun:

1. What is your price range? If you want to seriously attack the soil in your area and put in several hours per week, do not settle for a cheaper, less-powerful unit.

2. What do you want to hunt? Some folks chase coins, some like the beach, and some want relics from the past. Others are chasing meteorites, while others concentrate on gold nuggets, and only gold nuggets. Be honest with yourself; if you want "All of the above," admit it!

3. What type of unit do you want? Are you into new technology, or will you settle for tried and true? Do your research and figure out where your comfort level is. Some folks are happy to be the tip of the spear and adopt new technology first. Others like to watch and wait, to make sure it is the right evolutionary track to follow.

4. Practice, practice, practice! Jeff suggests that when you do settle on and bring home your new detector, you should remember all your best study habits and dive in. Read the manual. Review the video, if one is provided. Jump on the discussion boards. And then get into your backyard and practice. Learn the different sounds with some test targets that you know—bottle caps, rusted steel, coins, etc. You are basically tuning your ear. And it takes time.

Jeff has a good page of links to additional sites. He has done an excellent job of making a one-stop shopping source, but the truth is, it never hurts to hear the same good advice over and over.

Go Metal Detecting
http://gometaldetecting.com

This is another site filled with general information. Here is their top tip for beginners, and it should sound familiar if you remember Gator Girl's advice in chapter 1: Join a club!

"First we would suggest that you join a metal detecting or treasure hunting club. You will learn a lot more, a lot quicker, from other club members then you would by yourself! You will also find new friends, share your finds, and get support for the hobby. For some people, it is easier to hunt with a group than by yourself. If you are looking for a partner, you will find one there. Most clubs will let you come as a guest. Visit several to find the right one for you. You can even join more than one if you want to."

The site had plenty more common sense advice. It is a great spot to bookmark.

Metal Detector Reviews

http://metaldetectorreviews.net

This site works hard at staying up to date and relevant, and it will help you do your research on what unit to consider. You will find links to all the major manufacturers, tips about where to go, an active forum, and an FAQ, among other features. There is a lot of research rolled up into one good address. You will find some solid, basic information on selecting a detector to hunt for gold:

"If you live in an area where gold was found in its natural form, it's wise to buy yourself a detector specifically designed to locate small nuggets. The general-purpose detectors will locate bigger size nuggets, but those are far and few between these days. . . . But lots of small nuggets is a whole lot better than none. These specialty detectors are not cheap, but you get what you pay for. It may not be a bad idea to meet some local detectorists in your area and learn what detectors they use before parting with your hard-earned cash. The soil conditions could be a problem for some metal detectors, so do some research or consider joining a local club first."

The site provides reviews for three top gold nugget detectors: the Minelab GPX-4500 (about $5,000,) the Fisher Gold Bug 2 (about $850), and the White's Gold Master GMT (around $800). There are good insights into each unit.

At http://metaldetectorsreview.net/metal-detector-resources/how-to-get-started-metal-detecting.html, there are some videos and more excellent advice. Here is something worth emphasizing:

"Before going out to look for treasure with your new metal detector, it is advised to read the manual. Practice using your metal detector at home, and learn how to make adjustments as needed."

Metal Detecting World

http://metaldetectingworld.com/how_to_metal_detect_p1.shtml

This is another great site that is packed with information. "Sergei from Upstate New York" is a decent writer and an enthusiastic hobbyist. You will find his take on the usual basics, from basic map research to a nice glossary. Here is another site with some specific advice—let's see if you notice a theme:

"A metal detector can do amazing things, but it can also confuse and disillusion you if you do not understand its 'language.' You MUST know how to operate your detector to the best advantage and make proper adjustments under all search conditions as encountered. Start with thoroughly reading (several times) the instruction manual of your detector. As you begin detecting, and understanding of your detector grows, the quantity of recoveries will increase."

There is a link on the right side of this page where you will see "Where to metal detect." There are seventy different types of locales, and my guess is that you hadn't considered one or two of these. You probably had not considered old stone quarries, clotheslines, or around old roadside fruit stands, for example.

Treasure Barrel

www.treasurebarrel.com

Here is a great site, well written, with in-depth information you could spend hours devouring. Even better for our purposes, there is some specific information about gold nugget detecting worth considering:

"Ideally, a recreational detectorist would have two coils for metal detecting, a small 5"–6" coil and a medium/large 10"–11" coil for nugget hunting, as there are advantages to each size of prospecting coil. A larger coil allows for more ground coverage and deeper detection depth on larger gold nuggets, though the larger coil will likely lose some sensitivity on the smallest of targets.

"A smaller coil, often referred to as a sniper coil, will be limited on depth but tends to be more sensitive to the smaller picker and grain-sized gold nuggets. The smaller coil is also more maneuverable in heavily vegetative environments and can better scan into crevice areas and around rocks and boulders. For tight spots, an elliptical coil can perform better than a round coil."

I liked the in-depth research here, as well as strong advice for gold enthusiasts. There are articles entitled "How to find gold in a river," "51 Gold Nugget Hunting Tips," and "Metal Detecting for Gold Nuggets." Check each article out and get comfortable with the concepts *before* you buy a detector. But if you already received a device for a gift, some of the tips and tricks should still pay off, and you might find enough "treasure" to finance the detector you really want.

This site has a good collection of useful links as well.

Metal Detector Forums

Metal detecting is one of those hobbies where enthusiasts are more than willing to share what they know with beginners, and the conversations are full of great advice. Enjoy your initial status as a "newbie" and "lurk" for a while; in time you should be a full, participating member. Here are four forum links.

Detector Stuff
www.DetectorStuff.com
   Good active forum and industry links.

Metal Detecting Forum
www.MetalDetectingForum.co.uk
   More for Europe and the United Kingdom.

Treasure Hunting
www.THunting.com
   Good forums and articles.

Treasure Quest
www.TreasureQuestxlt.com
   Packed with information.

Metal Detecting Secrets
www.metaldetectingsecrets.com
   Cody Smith is a treasure-hunting expert with a simple credo: Proper Research + Proper Technique = Success! He offers a reasonably priced series of videos, covered by a $37 fee that gets you access to newsletters, videos, a book, and more. He is very serious about sharing his knowledge; here is a sample of what he offers:
   "In these videos you will learn everything you need to know to be ready before you step foot on a hunt. I'll show you how to classify an area, use geographic land features as clues to what is in the area, and how to systematically begin your search!"
   There is a money-back guarantee, so you do not have much to lose.

Factoidz.com
http://factoidz.com/getting-started-in-metal-detecting
   This site is not as packed with information as some of the others, but it has a good overview and some nice write-ups, including this advice about beginner's units:
   "Like with many hobbies, metal detecting becomes more fun once you learn more about it and how to use your metal detector. My friend

Solving the Black Sand Riddle

Bryon Tolle invented the Black Gold Magnetic Separator, a device for removing black sand from gold-bearing pay dirt. His invention was a big hit on the first season of Gold Rush: Alaska, *and he has more designs in mind.*

I have always been interested in gold prospecting. In my 20s I started by panning for gold. In my 30s I had my first claims. Now in my 50s I have partnerships in about 1,200 acres in different locations in Oregon. For the last five years, I focused full time on gold mining, along with designing, testing, and building new types

of mining equipment . . . one of which is my Black Gold Magnetic Separator. I demonstrated my first prototype on Discovery's TV show, *Gold Rush: Alaska.*

Deciding to build a magnetic separator was a direct result of the old saying that "necessity is the mother of invention." I was testing several properties in the Cave Junction, Oregon, area for the gold-per-ton values in each yard of gravel. This required panning black sands until midnight every night. After a week, it was very clear to me that I needed a magnetic separator. But magnetic separators trap and lose lots of gold in the removal process. My theory was that minimal gold losses would occur if separation could take place when the feed material was in a constant "free fall state." My first prototype proved the theory to be true, and after two more prototype designs, I perfected a production model.

has found 2,000 coins and numerous rings in his first 170 hours of using his metal detector. He uses the Bounty Hunter IV and the Tesoro Compadre."

Alaska Mining and Diving Supply

www.akmining.com/mine/fisher_f75_metal_detector.htm

Alaska Mining and Diving Supply is a great spot for deals, background information, well-written stories, and more.

KellyCo Detectors

www.kellycodetectors.com/fisher/fishergold-goldbug2.htm

Good information on the Fisher Gold Bug, a solid detector that works for meteorites, gold, and coins.

Final Thoughts on Metal Detectors

You cannot beat the Internet for collecting good information an
viding it either free or at a great price. Whether you concentrate on   ⌐
nuggets, old coins, meteorites, relics, or whatever you can find, you have
a decent chance of success if you do the right research, stay patient, talk
to as many experts as you can find, and join a club or group as you dive
in. This is a well-developed hobby, with its own identify, set of ethics,
and enthusiastic advocates. Technological advances have made metal
detectors better than ever, and the advances just keep coming.

You may stumble on something truly extraordinary that gets you on
the evening news. Still, your real treasure may end up being the outdoors
exercise you get, the friends you meet, or the new locales you research
and visit. Mostly, have fun!

Homemade Contraptions

As the Internet continues to expand, the ability of recreational miners to
share information has grown by leaps and bounds.

Gold and Platinum Explorations (GPEX)

The experts at www.gpex.ca/homemade-gold-prospecting-tools.html
have developed a page of DIY, or "Do It Yourself," machines and devices.
There are plans for a trommel, sluice, rocker, dry-washer, rock saw,
and vacuum kit. Each plan comes in an Adobe Acrobat PDF file for
downloading.

At www.blacksandbox.com/projects/index.cfm, you can find plans
that turn a Super-Soaker squirt gun into a Super Sucker hand dredge.
This site has tons of content—products for sale, videos, links, lists of
public mining areas, and more.

Over at Dan Goldberg's Operation Gold site (www.operationgold
.com), you can scroll down to a link for both of Sam Radding's books of
plans. He has devised homemade scopes, crack hooks, fanning boards,
suction sticks, portable sluices, and much more. In addition, this is a
great site for general gold prospecting information. There is a write-up
for Gold Panning 101, for Gold Prospecting 101, and a hugely popular
article on gold-panning vacations.

Chris Ralph is a prolific, knowledgeable miner, gem hunter, writer,
speaker, and mining engineer. His Nevada Outback pages also contain
loads of information about all the different aspects of mining, including building your own dredges and sluices. There is way more content

than you can go over in a day. Check out http://nevada-outback-gems
.com/design_plans/DIY_dredge/Homemade_dredge.htm for his dredge
construction advice. Scroll down to the bottom of the page for tons of
links too.

Arizona Gold Prospectors (www.arizonagoldprospectors.com/diy
.html) has an excellent page of links to building your own equipment.
Some of the links may be expired by now, but it is worth checking out.
One of the main places the Arizona site points to is Bill Wescott's old
Minin' Gold page at http://miningold.com/dnld.html. Bill has plans and
instructions for gold suckers, sometimes called gravel pumps, which
resemble giant snuffer bottles. These are ideal for pulling up gravel
without the hassle of a dredge, especially when you do not want to move
a likely looking rock and let all the gold roam free.

Sluice boxes are some of the oldest gold mining tools devised, after
gold pans themselves. Minin' Gold has three sets of sluice plans at
http://miningold.com/fineslu.html. There's a backpack sluice that can
be transported back into the wilds, an aluminum sluice with a pre-clas-
sifier, and a set of old wooden plans.

Minin' Gold also has a link to Jerry Bowen's mini-high-banker
plans, first published in the March/April 1995 issue of *Trails N' Tales,*
the United Prospectors Inc. newsletter. Their group is located in Vacav-
ille, California. The plans include lengthy step-by-step discussion and
good drawings.

Next there is a link to reprinted rocker box plans from Information Circular 6786, "Placer Mining in the Western United States," by E.
D. Gardener and C. H. Johnson. The US Bureau of Mines published this
document in September 1934. At this point of the Great Depression, hundreds of miners had headed back to the known gold districts of the West
to "make beans" the old-fashioned way. The circular helped them create
cheap, efficient gadgets.

In today's electronic, machine-mad age, where the drone of a gaso-
line engine is a sign of industry, there is something very soothing about
one man running a rocker box. It is quiet and clean, and generally no
permits are required to operate one.

Says the web page: "More gravel can be handled per man-day by rocking, or cradling as it is sometimes called, than by panning. Moreover, the
manual labor of washing a cubic yard is less. The same method of excavating the gravel is used whether it is panned or rocked. The rocker, like
the pan, is used extensively not only in small-scale placer work but also

in sampling and for washing sluice concentrates and material cleaned by hand from bedrock in other placer operations."

There's a page supplied by Mad Dog for the creation of a specific gravity scale. We all know that gold is nineteen times heavier than water, right? Well, what would it mean if your gold nugget were only fifteen times heavier? That computes to 15 grams per cubic centimeter and means your gold is only about .780 fine. The plans are not simple, but they are worth checking out.

Here are two more sites with ideas worth reviewing:

1. Free Print docs: http://printfu.org/free+gold+sluice+plans

2. Bucket classifier: www.coloradoprospector.com/EquipmentPlans/Classifier.html

METEORITE HUNTING

First, a little science background is in order for those who have not thought much about the earthly remains of shooting stars. There are three different types of meteorites: iron, stony-iron, and stony. Guess which two are the easiest to find with a detector? Yep, you guessed it: You need iron. The stony meteorites, referred to as chondrites,

PHOTOGRAPH BY SUZANNE MORRISON

Large Sikhote-Alin nickel-iron meteorite for sale at www.aerolite.org

sometimes contain little or no iron and are almost impossible to locate electronically. That makes them least interesting to detectorists but absolutely worth knowing. You will need to rely on visual clues to find these rocks, so you'll need a book with excellent photography. Your best bet is to pick up a copy of Geoffrey Notkin's book *Meteorite Hunting: How to Find Treasure from Space,* available at http://meteoritehunters.tv.

Iron meteorites, such as the Sikhote-Alin specimen shown in the photo, are what you normally think of when you conjure up an image of a chunk of space rock. They are massively heavy, and they always contain nickel. By contrast, nickel is not present in common iron, slag, and other metal chunks that are often mistaken for meteorites.

Meteorite Man

Geoff Notkin is a man of many talents, including writer, speaker, musician, and producer. He is perhaps most famous for his role as one of the Meteorite Men on the Science Channel.

My fascination with meteorites began as a child. I grew up at the southern edge of Greater London and spent my free time, aged 6 or 7, clambering across piles of debris in abandoned chalk quarries, looking for fossils and interesting rocks. My father was an amateur astronomer and instilled within me a love of the night sky. I was a very active kid, always collecting things, building things, examining bits and pieces I'd found under the microscope, and my long-suffering mother needed to find ways to keep me occupied. A popular destination for the two of us was London's Geological Museum, where I passed blissful afternoons gazing at rows and rows of mineral-laden cabinets.

Over time I discovered the Hall of Meteorites, and that is where my journey really began. I was amazed, almost entranced, by the meteorite exhibits. Yes, they were rocks, but they were rocks not of this Earth. Somehow, everything I loved as a little boy—rocks, minerals, astronomy, space exploration, science fiction, mystery, and adventure—seemed rolled up and encapsulated within these visitors from outer space. I promised myself, aged 7, that one day I would own a meteorite myself.

Many times, iron meteorites look like a hardened piece of clay that someone has pressed his finger against over and over. These little impressions are called regmaglypts and are unforgettable. Another basic identification tip is the fact that fresh iron meteorites leave no streak, although most finds have weathered and thus have a rusty coating.

Another common test is to see if your suspected meteorite attracts a magnet. Most meteorites attract a magnet easily, and many stony meteorites will weakly attract a magnet on a string.

Finally, the appearance of meteorites is often quite striking. During descent through the atmosphere, the space rocks develop a fusion crust that is black or dark brown, and it can be very distinctive.

So basically meteorites have three telling characteristics:

1. heavy

2. magnetic

3. fusion crust

If you slice, polish, and etch a meteorite surface, you should see the classic Widmanstätten pattern, as shown in the photo:

Sliced and etched meteorite fragment showing the classic diagonal lines of a Widmanstätten pattern

Where to Find Meteorites

As any experienced gold prospector already knows, gold is not just where you find it; gold is also usually where others have found it. Meteorites follow a similar pattern, except the known areas are called "strewn fields."

If you have ever seen a shooting star, you know that objects almost always come into Earth at an angle rather than straight on. When a large meteorite hits the Earth, or explodes above it, the distribution pattern is usually a large ellipse. That is the strewn field, and it can cover 500 square miles or more.

The main point for meteorite hunters is that you will have the most success finding a meteorite near where others were found. Several books offer maps for would-be sleuths. One good reference is *Rocks from Space: Meteorites and Meteorite Hunters* by O. Richard Norton.

Basically you are looking for some of the most inhospitable places on Earth: desert floors, Antarctic glacier fields, the Australian outback—anywhere that a strange rock would appear to be out of place, and not rust away to nickel-rich red powder in twenty years.

How to Hunt for Meteorites

There are three main ways to hunt for meteorites:
1. by sight
2. with a magnet
3. with a metal detector

We will go through each method in turn.

Hunting Meteorites by Sight

It takes plenty of practice and a sharp eye to learn how to identify the black fusion crust of a meteorite. You need to study what the different stony meteorites look like. They are much more common than the classic iron meteorites but harder to identify. Remember the advice from Gator Girl in chapter 1? To start honing your eye, you need to look in books, go to museums, attend club meetings, and really expand your network.

A great reference to consider is the *Field Guide to Meteors and Meteorites* by O. Richard Norton and Lawrence A. Chitwood.

Hunting Meteorites by Magnet

As noted earlier, many meteorites have at least a little nickel-iron in them and are thus attracted to magnets.

There are several high-end specialty magnet vendors online, including www.Magnet4less.com, www.duramag.com, www.kjMagnetics.com, and www.rare-earth-magnets.com. These sites sell high-quality permanent magnets with ten times the strength of an old ferrite magnet; they are tougher too.

Since rockhounds visit a lot of gravel bars in the course of rockhounding, and gold seekers handle quite a bit of material in the course of gold prospecting, it is likely you have passed over a valuable piece of space debris. If you have not caught meteorite fever yet, visit the *Meteorite Men* website (http://meteoritemen.com) and check out the stories there.

In one episode, the two meteorite hunters traveled to the Atacama Desert in Chile to visit a known "strewn field" where they had found fragments in the past. On other shows they had used metal detectors for their work, including one time when they rigged up a giant 10-foot array detector that they towed behind them in a Kansas wheat field. They found a huge space rock about 6 feet beneath the soil thanks to that contraption.

This time they rigged up a drag board fitted with dozens of powerful rare-earth magnets and hooked it to their pickup truck. They repeatedly raked the red desert floor and managed to attract dozens of little pieces of iron, worth between $5 and $10 per gram.

Before going further, you should be aware that these neodymium-based magnets are stronger than you are used to. The following warning is provided at www.UnitedNuclear.com:

"Neodymium magnets are very powerful, much more powerful than magnets most people are familiar with and need to be handled with proper care. The magnetic fields from these magnets can affect each other from more than 12 inches away. Please note that these magnets are fragile. Even though they are coated with a tough protective nickel plating, do not allow them to snap together with their full force or they

Giant neodymium-based ring magnet. You can see it has been dragged through the dust already and has picked up some magnetite, black sand, or iron.

Low-tech, Low-cost Magnets

If you want to put together a poor-man's meteorite magnet to drag through beach gravels or across a desert floor, you can take apart an old stereo speaker, grab some wire, and hook yourself up fairly quickly. The problem is that most stereo magnets are actually very brittle and prone to breaking after a short amount of time.

To make your own low-tech magnet stick, purchase a used ski pole at the local Goodwill store and pick up a fancy magnet at one of the many online sources, such as www.magnet4less.com. Glue it, tape it, or use a screw to fix the magnet on permanently, and your magnet stick is complete.

The Putter-Mag

Here is an easy, inexpensive system to put together, as shown in the accompanying photo.

Used golf putter with various magnets attached to the head of the club and the big ringed magnet sitting on top. Total cost was about $40.

Famed comedian W. C. Fields once observed there were two ways to travel: first-class, and with children. You may sometimes feel the same way about camping. Kids are great fun, and opening up a world of science and discovery is a treat. However, the way they run around without any shoes, risking a rusty nail and subsequent tetanus shot, is enough to drive a parent, aunt or uncle, or grandparent crazy. You can justify dragging your putter magnet around the campfire a few times because you are sure to clean up a lot of rusty nails and other trash, serving as a one-person camp cleaner. At right is a typical haul from just a few sweeps. In the more popular forest service campgrounds, you can run a quick pass over the gravels where you park; you are likely to snap up quite a few nails from perilously close to your tires.

Trash, black sands, and hot rocks picked up around a typical developed campground fire grate. The nickel is for scale only; magnets do not pick up most coins.

may chip, break, and possibly send small pieces of metal flying on impact. Our magnets can easily bruise fingers, and the larger ones can break finger bones and even crush hands as they attempt to connect together."

On that same Atacama Desert episode of *Meteorite Men*, prospector Steve Arnold got his fingers pinched between two magnets, and he too donated blood.

Neodymium Magnet Information

Here are some more links and additional information about neodymium magnets, found at www.kjmagnetics.com.

Rare Earth

KJ Magnetics has some excellent background information you will need to study before making your purchase. As they say on their website, "Neodymium magnets are a member of the rare earth magnet family and are the most powerful permanent magnets in the world. They are also referred to as NdFeB magnets, or NIB, because they are composed mainly of Neodymium (Nd), Iron (Fe) and Boron (B). They are a relatively new invention and have only recently become affordable for everyday use."

Grades of Neodymium

N35, N38, N42, N38SH . . . what does it all mean? Neodymium magnets are all graded by the material they are made of. As a very general rule, the higher the grade (the number following the *N*), the stronger the magnet. The highest grade of neodymium magnet currently available is N52. Any letter following the grade refers to the temperature rating of the magnet. If there are no letters following the grade, then the magnet is standard-temperature neodymium.

Platings/Coatings

Neodymium magnets are a composition of mostly neodymium, iron, and boron. If left exposed to the elements, the iron in the magnet will rust. To protect the magnet from corrosion and to strengthen the brittle magnet material, it is usually preferable for the magnet to be coated. There are a variety of options for coatings, but nickel is the most common and usually preferred. The best nickel-plated magnets are actually triple plated, with layers of nickel, copper, and nickel again. This triple coating makes magnets much more durable than the more common single-nickel-plated ets. Some other options for coating are zinc, tin, copper, epoxy, silver, and gold. Gold-plated magnets are actually quadruple plated, with nickel, copper, nickel, and a top coating of gold.

Demagnetization

Unlike most other types of magnets, rare earth magnets have a high resistance to demagnetization. They will not lose their magnetization around other magnets or if dropped. They will, however, begin to lose strength if they are heated above their maximum operating temperature, which is 176°F (80°C) for standard N grades. They will completely lose their magnetization if heated above their Curie temperature, which is 590°F (310°C) for standard N grades. Some magnets are made of high-temperature material, which can withstand higher temperatures without losing strength.

Visit www.kjmagnetics.com/neomaginfo.asp for more background information about neodymium magnets. Their glossary offers more details about magnets.

Meteorites and Metal Detectors

Magnets are relatively cheap and easy tools to use, but most serious meteorite hunters swing a metal detector as they work. Metal detectors have the advantage of peering beneath the top layer of soil, enhancing your hunt.

There are numerous manufacturers out there; here are links to the websites of two: Whites (http://whiteselectronics.com) and Fisher (www.fisherlab.com).

Antarctica has been a significant supplier of meteorites due to many factors, but primarily because the black rocks stand out against the snow and ice like a beacon. This link to the Armada Project will provide you with a lot of information about meteorites way down under: http://tea.armadaproject.org/caldwell/1.5.2003.html. Here is a snapshot of the project:

It is important to remember that only certain types of meteorites can be found with a metal detector. In particular, the ordinary chondrites, certain carbonaceous chondrites, and iron meteorites can be detected. Other carbonaceous chondrites, achondrites, lunar meteorites, and Martian meteorites do not contain enough iron metal to produce a response. Thus, there is an inherent bias in the meteorites that one can find with a metal detector. Even for the meteorite types that can be detected, it is not as easy to find them as some people think. The metal detector produces a constant hum, not unlike that of a small fly in your ear. The pitch and volume of this hum increases when a metallic object is under the detector's coil. Because of the wide variety of rock types in the moraines the ground balancing can only cancel out some of the rocks. Other mineralized rocks, known in the metal-detecting world as 'hot rocks,' will still produce a signal on the metal detector. Thus, metal detecting requires a lot of concentration. You have to listen to the audible signal of the detector, examine every rock that produces a signal to determine if it is a meteorite or a hot rock, and keep your eyes open for any interesting meteorites that the metal detector cannot find. On the other hand, metal detecting in Antarctica is much easier than in most other places in the world for one reason: there is no trash out here!

The metal detector has been used in every moraine that we have searched this season, with varying degrees of success. On one day, we hit a large concentration of ordinary chondrites and found twenty meteorites in the span of four hours. On other occasions, the metal detector had been used all day only to find one or two meteorites. Some areas are loaded with so many different types of hot rocks that it becomes impossible to find the meteorites among them. We have also covered ground that contained many meteorites, which for one reason or another did not produce a response on the detector. These meteorites were only found by painstakingly searching every square inch of the moraine on foot. In some areas we had to get down on our hands and knees to find tiny meteorites hidden among the other rocks in the moraines.

Getting back to the Meteorite Men, they had this to say on their website about their metal detector:

If you've watched the award-winning series *Meteorite Men* on the Science Channel, Discovery, Quest, or one of our other networks, then you've seen Geoff and Steve using the remarkable

Space Rock Detecting

Geoff Notkin is one of the Science Channel's Meteorite Men.

To be a successful meteorite hunter, you need to be dogged and determined. Meteorites are rare and valuable for a reason; they are tough to find. There are a few instances of people going out in the boonies and finding a new meteorite by accident, but they are few and far between. Meteorite hunting is a science, and the successful hunter must put in serious time, both in the classroom and in the field. The classroom part is research; you cannot expect to find meteorites, or any other kind of natural history treasure, if you are not sure what your prey looks like. It is crucial for the successful hunter to understand how meteorites fall, how they terrestrialize over time, and what they consist of. It is also vital that you know, really well, the equipment that will be used in the field. If you want to go searching with a metal detector, then practice in your garden first. There is nothing more frustrating than getting out in the field and realizing you do not know how to operate your own gear. At first you will find coins, bullets, and barbed wire and will begin to recognize the sounds made by different kinds of targets. Over time, you will do much better.

new Fisher F75. This extraordinary, top-of-the line detector is lightweight, perfectly balanced, extremely sensitive and the Meteorite Men's hand-held detector of choice. And it's a meteorite-finding machine.

The Meteorite Men used their F75s with great success at Canada's amazing Whitecourt Crater, at Gold Basin in Arizona, at the famous Odessa, Texas, meteorite crater, on the search for the legendary Tucson Ring, and at many other secret locations. If you want to up the odds of finding your own space rock, then you need to be using the best equipment out there, and that's the F75.

The cost is about $1,249. That's a little steep for most of us to justify to our chief budget officer, so they advertise a "starter" GoldBug for about $550.

White's GMT costs about $800. You can log onto their site (http://whites electronics.com/gmt.html) and get this report:

The White's GMT is a good choice for a low-end gold detector. By using the term 'low-end,' don't imply cheap quality, just low price. The GMT can be purchased for about $800 new and $500 used. It does have some problems with Arizona's heavily mineralized areas but can handle them decently with effort and practice. It can find gold as small as .02 gram with my experience and of course larger pieces. The fact that the GMT is a VLF, or very low frequency, detector means it can discriminate iron trash very well. In fact, from my experience I'd say the discrimination is 99.9% accurate on trash. The digital scale normally shows gold at 25 or lower. What I am referring to is the digital 'scale' called 'Probability of Iron.' . . .

More Meteorite Links

At www.whiteselectronics.com/tell/month/2003-february.php, there is a nice description of searching with a White's Goldmaster 4:

About an hour into the search we hit our first good target. My wife was doing the digging and about a foot down in an old dry streambed she uncovered what appeared to be an unusual shaped rock about the size of a large lemon and very heavy for its size. We debated on what it might be and even whether to keep it. Fortune was on our side and we took it home to have a local rock shop owner see if he could tell what it was. He determined that it was an "iron nickel" meteorite but advised we would have to have it analyzed by an expert in the field such as a university to determine its exact composition. We procrastinated for over a year before showing it to Dr. Jack Murphy, the Curator of Geology for the Denver Museum of Natural Science. He then asked us to send it to one of the world's foremost experts in meteorites, Dr. John Wasson of UCLA for further scientific examination. His study determined that it was a rare iron meteorite, almost in a class by itself. Some of its elements, besides iron and nickel, were gallium, iridium, arsenic, and yes, even a trace of gold. At our request, Dr. Wasson removed two slices of the meteorite, which we have donated to UCLA and the Denver Museum. Our Meteorite has been named the 'Cotopaxi Meteorite' and will be listed in the official meteorite registry maintained by the British Museum in London. The name 'Cotopaxi' comes from the area in Colorado near where we found our 'rock.' We soon plan on buying our second White's detector and our future searches will include meteorites along with gold.

At prices ranging to $100 per gram (or more), meteorites can be more valuable than gold, which at press time hovers in the $18 to $25 per gram range. However, prices depend on rarity, size, composition, and more factors, so don't get too excited. In addition, keep in mind that most meteorites are small in size. Do not fixate on the famed Willamette Meteorite, a seventy-ton behemoth revered by Oregon Indians and now on display at the American Museum of Natural History in New York City (www.usgennet.org/alhnorus/ahorclak/WillametteMeteorite.html).

Here are some additional meteorite links to follow:

Meteorites USA
www.meteoritesusa.com/meteorite-articles/wisconsin-meteorite-strewnfield-map/
Great information, and tons of links to keep you researching for days.

Meteorite Market
www.meteoritemarket.com
Claims to be the oldest and best place to buy meteorites.

University of New Mexico
http://epswww.unm.edu/meteoritemuseum/index.htm
Awesome museum.

Discovery
http://news.discovery.com/space/meteorite-impact-crater-google.html
Recent meteor crater found with Google Earth.

Wired
www.wired.com/wiredscience/2010/08/crater-hunting
Successful crater hunt.

Sahara Expedition

www.saharamet.com

Successful desert hunt.

University of Arizona

http://meteorites.lpl.arizona.edu

Plenty of info here.

Nine Planets

www.nineplanets.org/meteorites.html

Must be still counting Pluto; good collection of information and further links.

Space.com

www.space.com/18009-meteorite-collectors-public-lands-rules.html

Rules for what and where you can legally collect.

Additional Links

www.meteoritemarket.com/metid1.htm

Online key for "meteor-wrongs." Most supposed finds are actually common rocks.

http://radarmeteorites.wordpress.com

Up-to-date information about radar observations of meteor falls.

www.nuggetshooter.ipbhost.com/index.php?showtopic=19186

A forum of meteorite hunters who use metal detectors, discussing strewn fields.

CHAPTER 5
WHAT TO DO WITH IT

Once you bring home trophies from the field, you can start to experiment with preparing them for display or as gifts. If you find plenty of good material, you can even begin making jewelry. You will need to create some kind of work space—preferably a lab or shop.

TUMBLE POLISHING

One of the easiest ways to get started rockhounding is to collect agates, chalcedony, and other pretty rocks from creek banks, river bars, and ocean beaches. With the right water conditions, rounded rock is often abundant, and beginning rockhounds, often called pebble-pups, soon accumulate quite a bit of raw material. The most common next step is to tumble-polish the rocks for easy displays in attractive containers.

How to Tumble Polish Gemstones and Make Tumbled Gem Jewelry by Jerome Wexler is full of helpful information and a great book to get you started.

Tumble polishing is a controlled improvement on the natural polishing action of water. Instead of tossing specimens into the ocean surf, with an infinite number of different materials grinding away, the tumbler works on the principle of stages. Polishers work from stage to stage, increasing the grit number from 60 up to 1000, similar to the way carpenters use sandpaper. By using the coarsest grit at the beginning to knock off the big edges and then moving to finer and finer grits, the agates inside the tumbler become smoother and smaller. The process can take four weeks or longer, and it is not uncommon to have to repeat steps, stretch them out, or otherwise expand the time.

There are many commercially available tumblers, in varying sizes. The typical starting model is a Lortone 3A rotary rock tumbler, costing around $100. This unit sports a single three-pound barrel that takes the majority of the small rocks and pebbles collectors pick up. There are also dual-barrel models, six-pound models, fifteen-pound heavy-duty systems, and vibrating models.

Tumble polishers work constantly, 24/7, and generate a surprising amount of noise, especially on a quiet night. If you already have a work shed or lab, you should be fine. Tumblers can work in the garage, but they might need some noise dampening, such as a sound box. Also, spills are inevitable when polishing rocks. Seals can blow out or leak, spreading a nasty liquid that usually dries into a gray streak resistant to all but the most powerful household cleansers. Select an area that can withstand dirt, oil, and spills.

Typical Tumbling Procedure

Follow the instructions below to achieve the best results when tumble-polishing.

1. Prepare the sample. Before starting, sort your material so that you are not mixing rocks of unequal hardness. Most rocks in the quartz family—quartz, quartzite, agate, chalcedony, jasper, and petrified wood—are around 7 on the Mohs scale and can usually be mixed safely. However, some petrified wood is softer because it has become opalized and will grind away to shards if mixed with harder material. If at all possible, grind the same material in each batch—jasper with jasper, agate with agate, etc. You will get more uniform results that way.

2. You do not typically need to sort raw material by size. It's good to have different sizes so that your grit distributes better and polishes surfaces equally. For example, if you had one large piece of carnelian to polish, you could mix in small and medium agates as well to increase surface area contact.

3. If your rocks are particularly dirty, dusty, covered with seaweed or algae, or otherwise contaminated with organic material, wash them before tumbling. You can skip this step most of the time, but if you have too much contamination, you can build up gases and blow out the seal, causing a mess.

4. Load the barrel. The biggest temptation here is to jam the barrel full of material in order to start whittling down that big pile of raw material you have collected over the years. For best performance, however, your tumbler should only be one-half to two-thirds full when dry. Otherwise you put too much pressure on the small tumbler motor, and the raw material has less opportunity to shift around and grind.

5. Add grit. Next, add the grit to the raw material. For stage 1 this is usually 60/90 mesh grit, meaning it will fall through a #60 mesh. Stage 1 uses the coarsest grit and will knock off most of the material's corners and edges as you smooth away. Typically you would spoon in about four to six tablespoons of grit for a three-pound barrel, but consult the user manual for your particular tumbler. Purchase a used tablespoon measure at a thrift store so that you do not get in trouble for using clean kitchen utensils for this job. If you want to aggressively remove rough edges, tend toward the upper end of the grit scale. If you are only half filling your barrel and the material is already quite round, tend toward the lower end.

6. Add water. Now fill the barrel with water so that the tips of the top rocks are barely showing. If you do not add enough water, the grit tends to become a paste and is less effective. If you add too much water, you risk blowing out the tumbler's seals and also slowing down the process.

Preparing to rotate the tumbler, with note pad, screen, and the next grit lined up

7. Seal the barrel. With the material, grit, and water all inside, seal the barrel. Typically, a rubber lid sits atop the barrel, inside a lip. Then the metal lid comes down, followed by a washer and a plastic thumb tightener. You can hear air escape at the end of this stage, indicating you have a good seal. The tightener pulls up on the rubber seal against the metal lid, seating the rubber against the barrel. Shake the barrel slightly to ensure the grit does not clump up in the bottom of the barrel, and test the seal to make sure it is holding.

8. Record your work. Keep a small notepad and a pen nearby to write down what you are doing.

9. Set the barrel. With the tumbler plugged in and running, set the barrel on the rails and get started. You should hear the rocks rattling around in the tumbler.

You must keep good notes to make sure you are rotating your grit at the right intervals. NOTE: This tumbler was turned off during extended vacations.

10. Rinse and repeat. After at least a week, you are ready to repeat most of the above steps in the process. Remove the barrel from the tumbler and take it apart. This is best done outside in a spot that can handle the gray or rusty-red residue. Dump the barrel into a small screen, and wash it thoroughly to remove the spent grit and ground-up rock material. Set that aside and rinse out the barrel. Be sure to get all the old grit out, as you do not want to move to finer grit and have leftover heavy grit remaining to scratch your rocks. Return the rocks to the empty tumbler, hose down the area, and repeat the charging steps above.

11. Perform regular maintenance. Tumblers need continual maintenance involving three key concepts: cleanliness, lubrication, and belt tightening.

Never wash tumbler grit down your plumbing—it will soon clog the pipes.

- **Cleanliness:** Wipe off excess oil and debris periodically, and not just so you don't get dirty each time you inspect the device. Grime can build up and wear down moving parts.
- **Lubrication:** Constantly add lubrication in several key areas. Obviously the inside and outside of the revolving shafts need a drop of high-grade oil periodically, but there are other areas to check. Another prime spot is the shaft that emerges from the motor.
- **Belts:** Change the rubber washer belt annually. Constant usage stretches the belt so that it will start slipping under heavy loads. There is an adjustment nut that comes in handy early in a belt's life cycle, but as the belt ages and stretches, you will reach the end of the adjustment. One symptom to watch for in two-barrel tumblers is the inability to spin both barrels at the same time.

Always inspect your rocks before moving on to the next stage and a finer grit. Many experienced rock tumblers will tell you that they go through a lot more coarse grit than anything else. It is common to repeat stage 1 if the rocks have not rounded up enough. It is also common to run longer than a week to make sure you consume all the coarse grit.

Beginners make two common mistakes when tumbling rocks. The first mistake is to mix the wrong kinds of materials, which we discussed above. The second is impatience. Let the tumbler do its job! Wait at least a week between stages, especially stages 1 and 2. The grit needs enough time to grind away, and there is no sense in tossing out perfectly good grit because you're in a hurry. After a week there is not as much grinding going on, but the grit never completely disappears—it just gets finer. There is little harm in allowing the tumbler to run on stage 1 for a few days past the recommended one-week interval, other than making the rocks dizzy.

If you find there are now some very small rocks in your material, you can remove them and store them in a separate container. Anything less than 0.25 inch is not going to last much longer in the tumbler anyway. You can leave these smaller rocks in to help distribute the new grit, but it is more cost-effective to save them all and polish them together in a separate batch.

WARNING: Never wash your grit residue down the sink in your house. The material acts like a heavy, sticky sludge that quickly builds up in your pipes and requires expensive repairs to fix. Don't flush the residue down the toilet either.

Table 7: Tumbler Stages, with Notes

Stage	Grind	Grit	Notes
Stage 1	Coarse grind	60/90 Silicon carbide	Can be repeated as necessary.
Stage 2	Medium grind	120/220 Silicon carbide	One of these stages can be skipped. You are preparing for the pre-polish stage.
Stage 3	Fine grind	400/600 Aluminum oxide	
Stage 4	Pre-polish	1200 Aluminum oxide	Rocks should look nice when wet.
Stage 5	Polish	Aluminum oxide Tin oxide Cerium oxide	Expensive polishes work better.
Stage 6	None–Cleaning	Detergent	Even 30 minutes helps.

Example: Polishing Agates

Raw, rough carnelian agates from western Washington, ready to tumble at stage 1

Agates after stage 1

Agates at stage 3, with softer edges

Final polished agates

CARVING SOAPSTONE

When you think lapidary, you might be put off by all the tools and technology that are required or the investment in tools and raw material, but don't lose hope. If you have ever carved a grip on a wooden fire stick while shooting the breeze over a summer campfire, you have enough skill to work with soapstone. It is the easiest rock and gem material to get started with, and a $10 set of files plus a few sheets of sandpaper will have you busy in no time.

> **SAFETY ALERT:** If you have trouble with the sight of your own blood, are particularly clumsy, and your muscles are prone to ache or your fingers lock up, forget carving and move on. You will hurt yourself carving; the tools are sharp, and you will slip at least once. Your body can ache from holding a single position too long, and you may develop a blister. You may strain your eyes. Only you can judge the dangers against your personal limitations.
>
> Carving soapstone involves creating dust in the air and on your fingers and clothes. This dust frequently contains minor amounts of asbestos. You should always do your carving outside and create dust in the wind. Do not smoke when working with soapstone dust, sawdust, or other air contamination. Use your loupe to closely inspect the dust you create, and look for long stringy fibers that denote asbestos. Know the risks, and do not be reckless with your lungs.

In this section we will take it a few notches up from carving with a pocketknife and get some power tools involved. Primitive man can have his *Venus of Willendorf*, but we can do better.

Donal Hord

Now don't get the wrong idea. After reading this section, you won't be able to match famed sculptor Donal Hord of San Diego, who fashioned a young woman's head from obsidian and created the epic *Thunder* from nephrite jade.

Hord (1902–66) worked with the hardest woods and most difficult materials. He experimented with various rocks and

VENUS WILLENDORF

Reproduction of Venus of Willendorf, a type of fertility fetish popular in northern Europe after the last ice age. This example was carved in oolitic limestone and dates to 24,000 BC.

minerals, including granite, black diorite, obsidian, nephrite jade, and onyx. As a somewhat sickly and sheltered young man, he studied art in Mexico and developed a uniquely American style that celebrates the strength and nobility of ancient cultures. You can track his work via a website (www.artnet.com) that monitors art auctions to see if his art ever comes up for sale.

Here are a couple more Donal Hord–related websites:
www.sandiegohistory.org/hord/hordlist2.htm
http://en.wikipedia.org/wiki/Donal_Hord

Whatever your particular style, the part where art comes in is where you envision the form inside the rough material and see it before you carve it. You may not know it when you pick it up, or you may see it in a flash of light. For more insight into the artistic muse in all of us, you should meet Martin Schippers, aka "Dusty Fingers," an experienced carver in the Seattle area. You will get a good idea of how to succeed at your own, modest projects by understanding the steps he went through to create an abstract water fountain.

Safety Precautions

Talc is not asbestos, but they are both very soft. When you are around any metamorphic rocks that feel soapy and appear to be a greasy green or yellow, you could be seeing serpentin*ite*—a mélange of up to a dozen different types of serpen*tine*, and all related to soapstone. Even if you are just rubbing the material to a smooth state, you run the risk

PHOTO COURTESY OF MARTIN SCHIPPERS

Be extremely wary of getting soapstone dust in your lungs or eyes.

of harmful particles invading your blood stream and your lungs. You are far better off working outdoors. Always use caution and ensure that you have excellent ventilation. If you are going to operate sanders, grinders, drills, and power saws, you should always use a mask and eye protection, such as shown here, and maybe shin guards and a helmet if possible. Enough on safety tips; you have been warned.

Mineralogy Lesson

Soapstone is a talc-rich schist and has been fashioned into jewelry and tools for centuries. On the Mohs hardness scale, talc is a 1. There isn't really a chemical formula for soapstone—it is basically any material that is lower than 2 on the Mohs scale, which is your fingernail. The more talc present, the softer the stone. Wikipedia notes that soapstone occurs when tectonic plates grind against each other at great depth. The heat and the pressure, when mixed with the strange witches' brew of chemicals that circulate miles below the crust, is never quite enough to completely melt the rock, so it retains all its streaks and swirls.

Continuing the geology lesson into mineralogy, soapstone can start out as dunite or serpentinite, but with more metamorphism it cooks into a composition of talc, chlorite, and amphiboles, with trace to minor iron and chromium. Pyrophyllite is similar to soapstone and has similar uses.

Soapstone pipes are occasionally found among Native American artifacts, but catlinite, or pipestone, was apparently the preferred medium for fancy ceremonial purposes. As a side note, check out Pipestone National Monument at www.nps.gov/pipe. You have to be a member of a tribe and make reservations far in advance to dig there. So stick with soapstone!

Ten Easy Steps

Listed below are ten variable steps to follow when completing a soapstone-carving project.

Step 1: Find a rock.

There are multiple soapstone locales in the United States, which you can track down using Mindat at www.mindat.org. Outside Seattle, Washington, on the North Cascades Highway, the rivers and creeks near Marblemount contain some good soapstone material, and most of the mines are no longer active. That is the general area where Martin collected from, plus another chunk from a Washington State Mineral Council (WSMC) field trip at Lake Wenatchee. If you want further information, consult the Council at their new home page: www.mineralcouncil.com.

There are also collecting areas on Catalina Island, California; in southern Oregon; in Wyoming's Wind River Range; and in the Uinta Mountains in Utah, just to name a few.

Step 2: Envision the form.

If you do not already have something in mind, you now need to figure out your end game. Martin explains, "I don't know where it really comes from, but you just start to see something in there. I had a small boulder once that I just knew was going to be a frog, and out it came. I carved some salmon once, and it just seemed like the most natural thing to do with the pieces. After a little experience, you see something and you just know you could get a small orca out of it."

The accompanying figure shows a lizard that "appeared" out of a larger piece of material.

Animals and figurines are more of a challenge, so you might want to start with easier projects. When carving simple shapes and abstract forms, there is more leeway in the approach. You may simply want to work with the stone and experiment. It takes practice to learn the art of the possible, so feel free to try different tools and approaches.

Envisioning the form that you are about to release is the tricky part.
PHOTO COURTESY OF MARTIN SCHIPPERS

As Martin explains it, "Basically you're going from big to little. I'm sure just about anything used to shape wood or metal could be employed. A flat screwdriver and a carpenter's hammer would remove a lot of rock."

Here are some more examples of what would-be artisans are able to do with smaller chunks of material.

Roughed-out soapstone amulet

Sea turtle marked up and ready to go

Stylish swan ready to polish

You can fashion something fairly simple in very little time when working with soft stone. Like everything else about collecting geological specimens, what you do next, and where you go, is up to you. Soapstone carving can quickly become very tool intensive.

Files and sandpaper used to fashion small soapstone carvings

Finished round trinket fashioned from Catalina soapstone

Step 3: Cut off big chunks.

This is where the dust starts to fly, so be prepared to make a mess. Your main goal is to reduce the amount of time in later steps when you have to be more careful with trimming. A reciprocating saw with a good blade will work really well. Some rockhounds bring a carpenter's saw into the field with them to cut out top-quality chunks of soapstone, so any saw will work. Power tools, such as those shown here, are certainly more fun.

Martin wanted to create an interesting fountain, so he needed to taper the top and leave plenty of room for his imagination. He sawed one side smooth and then roughed in some beginning forms for swirls and knobs.

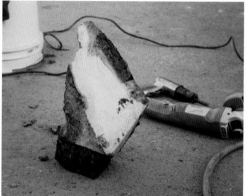

Use power tools such as a Saws-All to quickly remove big chunks of material.

Step 4: Rough out.

Martin uses a pneumatic grinder with rotary rasps for the rough stuff. In some cases, you might find that a chisel removes pieces more easily; if you have one, consider using one similar to that shown in the photo. This step is optional; the photograph is from a bowl project. He has a better collec-

An air chisel can help with material that will chip away. Marty used it more on the bowl project than on his fountain, so your mileage may vary.

tion of tools than most of us, so you never know if he really needed to use something or was just experimenting.

You should now have a good roughed-out form. If the piece will be sitting on a pedestal, you can get a flat bottom going. If there are arms or fingers, they should start to emerge. You should start to see your piece better at this point.

Step 5: Drill the hole.

Now that the form is roughed out and sits on a pedestal as shown in the photo on the next page, it is ready for the fountain hole. The drill bit for this fountain project was insanely long, requiring a good, straight aim, patience, and some luck. The fountain hole can be one of the trickiest parts to get right, because you sometimes have to drill the hole from the top *and* the bottom, which requires pinpoint accuracy. Martin's advice

PHOTO COURTESY OF MARTIN SCHIPPERS

PHOTO COURTESY OF MARTIN SCHIPPERS

is to invest in the longest bit you can buy, as the "two-hole" approach is maddening and can stop a project in its tracks.

Do not test the water flow at this point—the water may stain the raw soapstone.

Step 6. Fill any cracks.

Now that most of the rough stuff is over, it is time to repair the damage. Hopefully this step will be optional for you. If you sloughed off a piece when drilling, or otherwise saw a crack emerge, all is not lost. Invest in a few tubes of Superglue and get a good fill on the problem areas, as shown in the photo. Let the material dry for a minimum of what the label says. Be extra patient here, or you could have to repeat the step.

Drilling holes for a fountain requires the right bit and a lot of patience.

Step 7: Add detail.

At this point, Martin had zeroed in on the forms and shapes he wanted, including a line of grooves on the face. He roughed in the parallel lines with a mix of power tools, including a grinder like the one shown on the next page, and also used a set of files with various edges and tips.

Some material cracks more easily, but a strong glue will fix the problem.

"Just about anything will work," he says. "You can use a hobby rasp or file, a Dremel, some wood-carving chisels, smaller fine files, or a pocketknife. Avoid the temptation to grab anything from the kitchen."

Treat this step as the final work before fine sanding can start. Make sure you have taken enough material off; you do not want to rely on sanding to remove a lot of rock after this step.

Step 8: Start sanding.

At this point the form is definitely taking shape. He has put in a series of rough, parallel grooves, added various knobs and ridges, and worked with the piece's natural streaking from green to reddish. But the surface is still coarse, so sandpaper is the next tool.

A grinder is good for smoothing down the rough edges quickly.

"As far as the sanding goes, I start with 80 to 120 grit dry sand. It is pretty dusty, but that's why they call me 'Dusty Fingers.' When I get to 200 grit, I start wet-sanding, which simply involves keeping the sandpaper wet while working. I keep getting finer, going all the way up to 1000 grit. On a typical project, I wet-sand at 200, 400, 600, 800, 1000, and even 1200 grit."

Wet-sanding with a fine-grit sandpaper ensures that you do not take off too much material with each pass.

The next figure shows the wet-sanding step. By the way, look for the finer-grit sandpaper at auto body supply stores if you have trouble tracking it down.

This is the final step where you take material off, so make sure everything is nice and smooth before proceeding.

Step 9: Polish and seal.

Soapstone will turn color with age, water, dust, or other influences, as it will oxidize and form a crust. The best you can hope for is to slow down the process. There are several different schools of thought here, but Martin reports on what has worked best for him.

"I would recommend the urethane for a piece you plan to leave outdoors, and any water feature should have a satin or gloss finish. Indoor art would be better served with a carnauba-type wax, like for surfboards. The point being that fine art does not encourage a hard coating like urethane. It needs to be as natural as possible." Two different options are shown in the accompanying photo.

Step 10: Present the finished piece.

Here is the finished piece, without any tubes or pumps showing. From some angles it resembles a horse head, while from other directions it is more abstract. Martin simply calls the piece *Grooved Fountain.*

Minwax Helmsman spar urethane can be used to seal the sanded soapstone.

There you have it—ten steps to make an abstract soapstone carving with various tools. If you just want to make a fetish or an amulet, or some earrings, the process is a lot simpler, and fewer power tools are involved. Carving soapstone can lead to your working with additional materials, and you can see what experts do with material like jade. The fun part of this project is that you collected the material yourself. In addition, you can work at your own pace and learn something new. At

The finished product

some point you may even start to see salamanders creeping out of their rocky prison; then you will know you have achieved the rank of a master carver.

KNAPPING

Most rockhounds who have spent any time in the field report that it is common to come across a piece of jasper, flint, or agate that shows evidence of human activity. There is a characteristic seashell-shaped (conchoidal) fracture that usually requires a deliberate strike from a hammer stone. Often you will not spot the markings at the time, but upon getting home you will discover that a rock definitely has an amazing fit in your right or left hand. You might spot chips along the sharp edge, where it is clear that the rock had been a tool of some kind.

Consider ancient hand axes created by early tool-using humans. These were the Swiss Army knives of ancient man. A hand ax was often fashioned from a piece of cryptocrystalline quartz such as chert, agate, or jasper. With a few deft blows, such rocks could be crudely chipped to fit in a person's palm with a sharp edge showing. Hand axes could flay skin from a kill, break bones to reach the marrow, or even serve as a hand weapon. To view an amazing collection of hand axes used by prehistoric man dating back 200,000 years and more, check out www.sciencedaily .com/releases/2008/03/080311203247.htm. The site also has a link to human stone axes that date to 1.8 million years old: www.sciencedaily .com/releases/2011/08/110831205942.htm.

SAFETY ALERT: Knapping is dangerous for a variety of reasons: You are working with sharp edges, and, being human, you will eventually test an edge with your thumb and slice yourself. You will be striking rocks with other rocks or with tools, and chances are good that you will hit yourself at least once every hundred times. You will be creating dust, which you really don't want to inhale. You will send small shards flying into the air and, even more noteworthy, toward your face and eyes. Use good sense, try to work outdoors, consider wearing gloves, do wear eye protection, and pay attention to what you're doing.

Let's first talk about rocks and minerals on an atomic level. You are probably familiar with the concept of a crystal lattice—it's the way a mineral's atoms line up. Most of us have seen a sample crystal lattice for the mineral halite, common salt: sodium chloride. The chemical formula is NaCl. In a typical lattice, every other atom is the same, in every direction. Minerals such as halite have excellent cleavage; they shear along those planes perfectly and form little cubes with ease. These are not the minerals you are looking for to knap an arrowhead.

The best rocks for knapping do not cleave at all—they fracture. If you've ever seen what happens when a kid shoots a BB gun at a glass window, you know that characteristic cone-like fracture, called a conchoidal fracture. A conchoidal fracture is a curved fracture pattern characteristic of fine-grained rocks, especially obsidian, but also jasper, agate, chert, and flint. *Conchoidal* is derived from the Greek word for shell, and this type of fracture has smooth, shell-like convexities and concavities.

Clamshell on the left; classic shell-like fracture pattern in obsidian on the right

The fracture is random on a microscale, yet predictable at the macro level. When you cleave a mineral along its cleavage plane by striking it sharply at a logical angle, all that energy dissipates quickly as the mineral breaks apart cleanly. By contrast, in a conchoidal fracture pattern, the energy from your strike forms a small ball or bulb and then bursts through the material in fringes and hackles away from the strike, breaking along an impact zone. If you are a good knapper, you learn to make a succession of impact craters.

Online Knapping Resources
Check out the links below for some online knapping resources.

FlintKnappers
http://flintknappers.com
Multiple artisans; great stuff.

Sparrow Creek

www.sparrowcreek.com

    Beautiful artifact art.

Obsidian Arts

www.obsidianarts.com

    Tony Stanfield's knives and arrowheads.

Flint Ridge

www.flintridgeflint.com

    Gary Hardy's flint site.

Art of Ishi

www.artofishi.com

    Mike Cook's art.

Ore-Rock-On

http://orerockon.com/knappers.htm

    Tim Fisher's source for prized obsidian varieties.

Paleo Rocks

www.paleorocks.com

    Great source for flint.

Neolithics

www.neolithics.com

    Flint knapping supplies.

Flint Knapping Tools

www.flintknappingtools.com

    Kits and supplies.

Native Way

www.nativewayonline.com

    Supplies, kits, books, and DVDs.

Novaculite

www.novaculite.com

    Prized source material.

Puget Sound Knappers

www.pugetsoundknappers.com
Outstanding group dedicated to knapping.

Artifact Grading

www.artifactgrading.com
Native American authentication service.

Tools

The experts describe three different types of knapping:

1. Hard hammer percussion

2. Soft hammer percussion

3. Pressure flaking

In most beginners' kits you will receive the four tools shown here:

- Abrader—Roughs up thin edges to knock off bigger pieces.
- Copper nail—Works as a pressure flaker to do more detail work.
- Leather pad—Protects clothing from cuts and slices.
- Copper "bopper"—Knocks off bigger pieces for soft hammer percussion.

Knapping tools. From top left: abrader, pressure flaker, leather pad, and copper "bopper."

Puget Sound Knappers member Mick Hill pounded out this double-edged ax head in about 45 minutes. Check their website at www.pugetsoundknappers.com/how_to/how_to.html for plenty of "how-to" information.

Knapping and Rockhounding

James A. Miller is not only a member of the Puget Sound Knappers but also a member of the Washington Prospectors Mining Association. If you subscribe to *Rock & Gem* magazine, you may also have read his material. The knappers' "resident geologist," he has a gallery of specimens made from rock from all over North America, such as the following:

- Split base ensor point made from China Hollow, Oregon, jasper
- Cumberland point made from obsidian
- Dardanelle point of quartzite from the Spanish Diggings in Wyoming
- Dalton point in yellow kaolin flint
- Hernando point from moss agate
- Clovis point in dacite
- Lancelot blade in jet-black chert
- Kirk point in translucent Swedish flint
- Montell-style point in red jasper
- Snyders point in novaculite
- Andice point in Burlington chert

Jim also sells an amazing little electronic book with great research into knapping materials. *The Flintknappers Guide to Rock*, shown in the figure, costs $12. You can find a link at www.flintknappers.com.

PHOTOS COURTESY OF JAMES A. MILLER

Jim Miller's book contains amazing pictures of different styles of knapping and the different materials he used for true rock art.

Various arrowheads and fancy points from Miller's book

PRESERVING FOSSILS

When fossils are silicified, or turned to agate, they have their own protection from the elements and need little in the way of additional preservation. That's not true for most leaf fossils or for shells encased in sedimentary rock. They are crumbling already and will soon be hopelessly rotten, as is the case in the photo. Too often, your job as a fossil hunter is reduced to search and rescue.

This fossil gastropod will be hard to rescue.

Using PVA on Fossil Shells

Fortunately there are chemicals to bring to the battle. The primary chemical is Vinac (polyvinyl acetate), shown in the top photo on the next page and available from the Black Hills Institute, a foremost authority on fossil preservation. You can buy it here: www.bhigr.com/store/product.php?productid=262.

Here is some advice from the institute:

Polyvinyl acetate, commonly known as Vinac is a great high-quality preservative coating that can be used in all stages of fossil collecting and preparation. We use high-purity, Polyvinyl Acetate Beads (PVA) from McGean Rohco, as a penetrant and coating for fossils in both the field and in the laboratory. We dissolve these odorless,

Mix acetone and PVA outdoors, where the fumes are less dangerous

tasteless, nontoxic beads in acetone (approximately one pint of PVA beads per gallon) to make a thick concentrate. This is later thinned with additional acetone for different viscosities

The fossil on the left is dull and untreated; the one on the right has been brushed with a light coat of PVA.

These Miocene shells from the Astoria Formation near Newport, Oregon, all have a thin layer of PVA on their shells.

for various uses. Thicker solution will work best to slow the weathering if a specimen must be secured for later excavation and extraction. Thinner solution will leave a light protective coating on the surface of prepared fossils. PVA is probably one of the finest consolidants for porous materials or for a flexible coating on fossils. PVA can also be dissolved with water to create a white glue (similar to children's school glue) or with a 50/50 solution of acetone/ethyl alcohol or even pure ethyl alcohol to create a substitute for "Butvar." We are a distributor of McGean-Rohco's PVA beads for quantities needed in pale-ontology and a variety of other uses.

Coal Balls

In many midwestern US coal fields of the Pennsylvanian period, nodule-like balls of plant remains are cast aside, as they do not contain enough plant material to rate as even poor coal. Composed of calcium carbon-ate, they often contain other minerals, such as iron pyrite and magne-sium phosphate. They enable paleontologists to study the anatomy of various fossil plants, and there is a technique called a "peel" that reveals intricate detail.

According to the write-up at the Ohio University website (www.ohio .edu/plantbio/staff/rothwell/pbio460-560/Coal_Ball_Peel_Technique .htm), it is possible to treat these coal balls and peel off a slim layer. You'll need a coal ball, a saw, some 5 percent hydrochloric acid, a glass plate, #600 grit carborundum, acetone, and a sheet of acetate.

Read these steps carefully before starting:

1. Cut the coal ball with a diamond-bladed saw so that you have one smooth, flat edge.

2. Grind the flat surface of the coal ball slab to a smooth, even finish using #600 grit carborundum and water on a glass plate. This can get messy; don't splash the grit onto your good clothes.

3. Rinse the smooth surface thoroughly in running water. It should already reveal some interesting patterns and textures.

4. Etch the surface by holding it for about 20 seconds submerged in 5 percent hydrochloric acid. (This will not harm the skin of your hands.)

5. Rinse the surface carefully under running water. Do not touch the surface!

6. Dry the surface in air for several minutes. Be patient at this step so that you don't have any water remaining to dilute the acetone you apply next.

7. Support the coal ball in a gravel box or in a sink so that the surface is level.

8. Flood the surface with acetone.

9. Apply a piece of cellulose acetate (precut to the proper size) directly onto the acetone-wet smooth surface. Roll the acetate across the flat surface as you apply it so that you don't trap any air or create any bubbles.

10. Allow the film to dry for at least 20 minutes, and then peel it from the surface. The result is an image much like the figure shown here, which was scanned at high resolution.

Thin section of a peeled coal ball, scanned at 2400 dpi

The acetate sheets can be ordered from multiple sources on the web; first try Dick Blick at www.dickblick.com/products/grafix-clear-acetate-sheets-and-pads.

Breaking Concretions

Getting to the prize inside a concretion is rarely easy, but your reward could be a beautiful, highly preserved fossil fern or a fossil crab.

Artificial Weathering

The safest method for breaking open concretions is the "freeze-thaw" method. Here is a quick rundown:

1. Soak your entire concretion in a plastic tub or small bucket for at least two days, preferably longer. It takes time for the water to invade the concretion, and you need to penetrate the concretion's natural bedding plane.

2. Place your tub, with water and the concretion still in place, into your freezer. Your container must be able to handle freezing, so light plastic is probably not a good idea. Also, remember that water expands when it freezes; and you don't want a mess in there with your food.

3. Keep the tub in the freezer for at least a week. You are hoping to expose a hairline crack in the concretion.

4. Remove the frozen concretion, and let it thaw out for a day.

5. Inspect the concretion to see if any cracks are starting.

6. If you see a crack starting, tap it with a light geology pick several times. Do not try to crush the concretion—you are merely trying to help natural forces along. If you're lucky, the concretion could split in half.

7. Even if you do not see a crack beginning to take shape, tap the concretion with a light geology pick in a spot where you *wish* a crack were starting. You could get lucky, but stop after a half-dozen attempts.

8. Repeat the freezing and thawing process as many times as your patience allows. Eventually you should see a crack start to form.

Mazon Creek

http://paleobiology.si.edu/mazoncreek/mazonPaleo.html

Mazon Creek–area fossils occur in siderite concretions, occasionally as compression fossils on shale. Here's what the Smithsonian National Museum of Natural History has to say:

> Once collected, concretions should not be hammered too vigorously; many a specimen has been shattered by an impatient collector. A light tapping may produce a crack which splits open to reveal an impression. However, if tapping fails, the concretions are best treated by the freeze-thaw method. They may be placed in plastic, water-filled pails over winter. The freeze-thaw process of the seasons over several years should open a good proportion of the concretions. Each spring, remove the open concretions from the pails. For those who are less patient, quicker method is to place the concretions in sturdy water filled containers such as plastic bleach or anti-freeze bottles. A few days in the freezer, a few days out to thaw. Check the contents after several thaws and remove the opened concretions. About a dozen such sessions are usually sufficient. Concretions still unopened are best left to the wallop technique, mentioned above.

Ammonite Concretions on YouTube

Waiting for Mother Nature just takes way too much time for the Canadian ammonite hunter in this YouTube video: www.youtube.com/watch?v=XJ0VCEvuvrA.

By Microwave

If you have an old microwave that you won't worry about being chipped by a flying rock, and you are absolutely certain there is no pyrite or other metal in your concretions, you can move the weathering process along by microwaving them. You can heat them up quickly, drench them in ice water, and repeat the process at will.

Prepping Crabs

Prepping crabs from hard concretions takes a lot of time and patience. From the accompanying figure, you can also see that it's dusty work.

A Dremel tool or engraver won't last long; you need to invest in an air scribe. But the result, as shown here, can be well worth it.

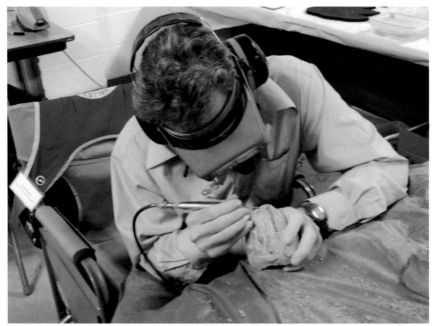

Protect your lungs from dust when attacking fossil specimens with power tools.

Crab
Pulalius vulgaris

Age:	Eocene
Formation:	Lincoln Creek
Location:	Grays Harbor County
	Washington, USA
Reference:	Rathbunn, 1908

Prepping fossil crabs from inside large concretions can be very rewarding.

If you do a web search on "preparing fossil crabs," you'll find several links. Here are just some of them:

Jason Boddy
www.fossilcrabs.com
Will take commissions!

Black River Fossils
www.blackriverfossils.org/USA/Virginia/WestmorelandCounty/tabid
/53/TripReports/3570/Default.aspx
Eastern crab fossils.

Terra Fossils
www.terrafossils.com/Crustaceans%20angl.htm
Many crab fossils for sale.

Fossil Pictures
http://fossilspictures.wordpress.com/2009/03/19/harpactocarcinus
-punctulatus-eocene-italy
Italian crabs.

Sculpted Stone
www.sculptedstone.com/index.cfm?fuseaction=arc.sh_item&prod_id
=3371
Cretaceous crab fossils; Australia.

Pinterest
http://pinterest.com/richiekurk/fossil-crab-crustacean
Fossil mall.

Fossils for Sale
www.fossilsforsale.com/site_arc/index.cfm?action=item&prod_id
=326&
South American fossils.

Crystal World
www.crystal-world.com/html/fossils/fossil_preparation.htm
Fossil prep; big crabs.

Fossil Forum

www.thefossilforum.com/index.php/topic/5509-how-to-prepare-a
-fossil-crab

Good discussion.

YouTube

www.youtube.com/watch?v=U7y6ZTonT8Q

Video with Dr. Kirk Johnson and artist Ray Troll.

YouTube

www.youtube.com/watch?v=XeSMhOomxwQ

Time-lapse video revealing a decent crab.

Prepping Bones

Many top museums with big mammal and dinosaur displays also provide a window into their fossil prep labs. For example, at Southwest
Adventist University you can occasionally watch a "dino cam" as the
preparers work away: http://origins.swau.edu/projects/research/fossil/
prep/index.html.

From Botswana, this expedition updates its site often: http://expedition
live.org/category/feathered-dino-death-pit-expedition-2012.

Here's a YouTube video from the Museum of the Rockies: www.you
tube.com/watch?v=IISDj74vroM.

The next two figures show workbenches from Rancho La Brea in Los
Angeles and the Wyoming Dinosaur Center museum in Thermopolis.

The fossil prep lab at the
Rancho La Brea tar pits in
Los Angeles, California, is a
wondrous place to watch in
action.

A large dinosaur bone just arrived from the field and ready for prep at the Wyoming Dinosaur Museum in Thermopolis.

Ulrich's Fossil Gallery (www.ulrichsfossilgallery .com) is just outside Fossil Butte National Monument in Wyoming. Ulrich sells both fossil prep kits and fully prepped and mounted specimens, and offers dig-your-own quarry trips. Look at the accompanying figure for a view of one of their spectacular mounted fossil fish.

Ulrich's Fossil Gallery, outside Kemmerer, Wyoming, has one of the most spectacular displays of fossil fish from the Green River Formation. You can purchase a framed specimen or pay to dig at their quarry.

JEWELRY MAKING

One of the most common things to do with a prized piece of gem-quality material is to create some kind of jewelry from it. For thousands of years artisans have crafted earrings, amulets, bracelets, and more. Four examples appear on the next page. More recently, rockhounds have learned to create belt buckles, bolo ties, and more from cabochons (CAB-oh-shawns), convex, highly polished stones. There are hundreds of books available about jewelry making.

Four different types of jewelry made from fossils. From left: coral, amber, ammolite, and a trilobite.

There are several easy ways to create jewelry from your prized material, but most require tools and machinery if you are going to move very far beyond simple tumbling.

Stringing and Wire-wrapping

Look for a club or shop offering introductory classes if you want to get started. The Gem Faire folks host shows regularly; browse to www.gemfaire.com to find out when the next show will be near you.

For a popular, inexpensive starter book, pick up *The Basics of Bead Stringing* by Debbie Kanan.

Consider taking classes to get started stringing beads. You can also find numerous kits that will get you started quickly. The list below is the result of an Internet search for turning quartz crystals into jewelry. You will need to pick up tools such as those laid shown on the next page.

Etsy

www.etsy.com/shop/GiftbearerSupply?section_id=6192532

Lots of supplies for sale.

EHow

www.ehow.com/how_5217618_make-rock-quartz-crystal-jewelry.html

Turn quartz crystals into jewelry.

Silver Enchantments

www.silverenchantments.com/quartz-crystal-beads.html

Beads for sale.

Tools for beading

Beading equipment for sale

Fire Mountain

www.firemountaingems.com/encyclobeadia/beading_resources
.asp?docid=GMSTNPRPRTSRCKC

    All about quartz.

Mama's Minerals

http://mamasminerals.com/pages/How-To-Clean-Quartz.html

    Cleaning quartz.

Beading Daily

www.beadingdaily.com/media/p/172739.aspx

    Amethyst.

Sawing

Making slabs out of large pieces of prized material is quite a thrill; the pieces for sale in the figure on the next page are amazing. Again, going back to Gator Girl's advice earlier in this book, you should talk to experts at clubs, shows, museums, and rock shops before investing in your own equipment. Use the links below to track down new equipment, or do your own search to find used saws that still have some life left in them. You can often find used equipment for sale at rock and gem shows, as shown on the next page.

Ali Baba

www.alibaba.com/showroom/rock-saw.html

    Great virtual showroom.

Cigar Box

http://cigarboxrock.com

Saws and sphere machines for sale.

The Rock Shed

www.therockshed.com/equipment2.html

Barranca equipment for sale.

Lortone

www.lortone.com

Top equipment manufacturer.

Top 20

www.top20sites.com/Top-Rock-Saws-Sites.

Follow the links to suppliers.

Rock Tools

www.rocktoolsinc.com

Go Big!

Rock Saw

www.rocksaw.org

Big equipment for quarrying and fieldwork. You know you want one!

Slabbed material for sale

Used rock shop equipment for sale

Cabochons

The art of making cabochons dates to ancient times and has historically been used on material unsuitable for faceting. Pre-worked material comes in a variety of sizes and shapes and is for sale at numerous sites

Display of fashioned cabochons for sale

on the web. Two books to consider are *Cabochon Cutting* and *Advanced Cabochon Cutting,* both by Jack R. Cox. They are perfect to help you get started making your own cabochons.

Here are a few links to run down if you are considering creating your own cabs.

Bob's Rock Shop
www.rockhounds.com/rockshop/oplc_cab.shtml
Cabochon making 101.

Inland Lapidary
www.inlandlapidary.com/user_area/howtocab.asp
Great site for learning how to make cabochons.

Rio Grande
www.riogrande.com/Category/Gemstones/106/Cabochons/182
Large selection of cabochons for sale.

Gem Photographer

Robert Weldon is the photography and visual communications manager for the Gemological Institute of America, www.gia.edu, located in Carlsbad, California. He has been with GIA for about eleven years.

My mom was an amateur gemologist—while she never studied the science, she collected and read many books on the subject. When she was collecting gems, she often pondered whether they were natural or synthetic. As the mystery deepened for her, my desire to know the truth really led me to my career path. After obtaining a degree in business, I became the assistant manager at a jewelry store in Phoenix . . . which then led me to GIA and to earning my Graduate Gemologist diploma.

I am definitely a rockhound—my curiosity about gems often leads me to their place of origin. I've had the good fortune to visit many gem-producing countries in my travels throughout the world, and it never ceases to amaze me how much work goes into finding these rare gems that we enjoy so much. I have traveled to the emerald mines in Colombia, which produce some of the world's most amazing gems, and Myanmar (Burma), which mines sapphires and rubies. While I enjoy visiting the mining sites themselves, one of the perks is interacting with the people who do the mining.

PHOTO COURTESY OF ROBERT WELDON, GEMOLOGICAL INSTITUTE OF AMERICA

About.com

http://jewelrymaking.about.com/od/aboutmetalandstones/ss/092808.htm
All about making cabs.

YouTube video

www.youtube.com/watch?v=LgluzZrrpsg
Short how-to video.

Faceting

The top of the line for jewelry making is faceting gem material for setting into rings and other settings. There is a lot of math involved in order to allow the play of light through the crystal to illuminate the material, and jewelers must study long and hard to be certified. The top school in the United States for studying gem faceting is the Gemological Institute of America, or GIA, located in Carlsbad, California, just north of San Diego, and shown in the figure. Their website is www.gia.edu.

World headquarters for the Gemological Institute of America is in Carlsbad, California.

A good print guide to start with is the *Facet Cutters Handbook* by Edward J. Soukup. You'll also need a faceting machine and various accessories similar to the ones shown in the accompanying photos.

Faceting wheel

Tools of the trade for faceting

Student lab at the Gemological Institute of America

These can be a considerable investment, so again you are advised to talk with club members, rock shop owners, vendors, and other experts before plunging in.

If you find yourself hooked on faceting, you can attend one of the GIA's career fairs to learn more about the institute, or visit their career website at www.careerfair.gia.edu. If you get accepted into their program, you could find yourself learning in a lab environment similar to the one shown above.

If you just want to learn more about faceting, here are a few links to explore.

Gem Society
www.gemsociety.org/info/gemlore/gl_02.html
All about faceting.

Bob's Rock Shop
www.rockhounds.com/rockshop/gem_designs/index.shtml
Great place; diagrams.

Gem Cutter
www.gemcutter.com
Accessories for sale.

Faceter's Guild
www.usfacetersguild.org
    Loaded with information.

Best Cut Gems
www.bestcutgems.com/facetingmachine
    Machines for sale.

YouTube
www.youtube.com/watch?v=rVLjMgM1y7Q
    Interesting video about faceting sapphire.

Faceting Academy
http://facetingacademy.com
    Tons of information about faceting.

Precision Gem Cutting
www.precisiongemcutting.com/learn.html
    Offers classes for getting started and becoming proficient.

Metallurgy and Metalsmithing

It is beyond the scope of this handbook to provide detailed information about the field of metallurgy, or to guide you very far if you want to learn how to separate precious metals from black sand, ore, or electronic waste. There are chemical methods and temperature-based methods, and both are dangerous. The following websites offer background, information, and techniques.

Nevada Outback
http://nevada-outback-gems.com/Reference_pages/Amalgamation.htm
    The historic way to use chemicals to extract gold from black sands was to use mercury. It was dangerous. You can read about the story here, but there are far more interesting links on this site than just the amalgamation story.

Silver Supplies
www.silversupplies.com/catalog/new_product/testers.shtml
    A good place to purchase an electronic jewelry tester.

Finishing.com
www.finishing.com/336/16.shtml

An older forum taking a stab at "Gold Recovery for Dummies" using chemical methods.

eHow on melting gold
www.ehow.com/way_6001539_gold-melting-techniques.html

If you want to try your hand at melting down scrap gold, here's a place to find out how.

Mellen Company
www.mellencompany.com/Products/ Furnaces/Crucible%20Furnaces/CS%20 Series%20Crucible.htm

All about crucibles, such as shown in the photo, plus sales and information about kilns and furnaces.

Crucible for melting material at high temperature and pouring it into molds

Channel Advisor
http://stores.channeladvisor.com/ MakeYourOwnGoldBars/Molds%20 to%20pour%20Gold%20Bars/

Make your own gold bars using crucibles, molds, flux, and other supplies. You may need to crush your material first in something similar to the device shown in the bottom photo.

Mortar and pestle for crushing material into a powder

Bodyworkz Supply Co.
www.bodyworkzsupply.com/pm-nitric .html

An all-caps explanation of using the acid known as aqua regia to recover gold, silver, and platinum group metals. There is a good video series on YouTube; try Prospector Rick's silent video at www.youtube .com/watch?v=hURm6wpRY48. You will see a lot of related links on the left side of the page.

Microwave Gold Kiln
http://microwavegoldkiln.com/smelting_tips
Do not use your kitchen microwave!

Gold Sucker
http://goldsucker.com/blog/?p=26
Technical information about turning a microwave into a kiln. Check their video at www.youtube.com/watch?v=tB3oQeTG-Mc.

Gold in Russia
www.gold-rus.com/Gold/Microwave-Gold-Kiln-Kit.html
They make microwaving gold look simple.

Colorado Prospector
www.coloradoprospector.com/forums/index.php?showtopic=3266
Q&A on their forum about using your microwave as a kiln.

Ganoksin Project
www.ganoksin.com/listing/Category/rare_historical_Metalsmithing_ebooks

If you want to learn more about metalsmithing in order to create jewelry such as shown in the photograph, there are plenty of pages on the Ganoksin site. They have print books for sale, e-books, videos, articles, and tons more.

Large gold nuggets can be made into excellent jewelry by soldering a clasp onto one end.

Gold Palace
If you want to just purchase jewelry online, there are hundreds of sites that will take your money. Try www.goldpalace.com/gold_jewelry.htm.

DISPLAYING YOUR TREASURES
It can be very hard to "leave 'er right where you found 'er" if you remember getting skunked on your early trips. The more collecting trips you make, the more material you are likely to bring home. After a few years, you probably have piles of rocks throughout your yard, and you likely have crates and boxes gathering dust in the garage or basement.

Rockhound and Curator

Lara O'Dwyer Brown is the curator of the Rice Northwest Museum of Rocks and Minerals in Hillsboro, Oregon (www.ricemuseum.org).

I've always picked up what I deem to be "nice rocks" when I'm out and about. I love finding rocks that I can use to teach with. These days, as curator, I'm interested in finding good teaching specimens and rocks that would fit in our museum.

I first realized that I was attracted to studying the Earth when I was 12 years old. I enjoyed learning about the processes that shape the Earth, from glaciers to rivers, and was excited to observe landforms on Sunday drives in the Irish countryside with my family that reflected these processes. A trip to Sicily when I was 14, including a visit to Mount Etna, confirmed my passion for becoming a geologist.

If you want a job in a museum or as a curator, start volunteering now. Volunteering and gaining valuable museum/curatorial experience is highly regarded in this profession.

Maybe some young geology student could unravel the various "leaverite" specimens you keep outdoors. Your best treasures deserve better, and there are many products available to help you show off your collection. Trays, cabinets, and shelves are an obvious answer for starters, depending on your budget. Many other display aids lurk among your everyday household accessories, if you know where to look. In this section you'll find a few easy tricks for showing off your best geology specimens, from tumbler material to fragile fossils.

The "Rocktini"

Every rockhound has different materials they favor. Most are a big fan of the easiest tool there is—the tumbler. To start off, consider all those rocks you have been tumbling over the years. To show off some of your tumbled rocks, take a look at a prop you might have around the house—the old-fashioned martini glass.

To many older collectors, just the word *martini* speaks of a time when American cars were bigger and faster every year, when Frank Sinatra was shuttling between Los Angeles and New York and Las Vegas, and you measured someone by how much vermouth they allowed in their drink. Every few years martinis make a comeback, and you

Two "rocktini" glasses filled with polished Oregon sunstones and topped with a single red jasper

probably have a couple of those classic glasses in your kitchen or behind your wet bar. They are often available at flea markets and second-hand shops.

Start with a material that polishes to a clear or yellowish color. One excellent choice is common sunstones, which look like liquid drops of honey when polished. If you ever get the opportunity to travel to the premier sunstone-collecting locale in North America, the Rabbit Hills near Plush, Oregon, you are sure to come back with several pounds of small yellow sunstones. It would be a crime for them to sit in a baggie on the shelf when finished.

Instead, fill a martini glass close to the top with tumbled material, all of the identical color. Sunstones are great, but agates or chalcedony will also do. Small material works best for this display, to make sure the glass looks "full." But the real key is to make sure the color is identical. Then top off with a large piece of colored jasper, preferably green like an olive. Red will also do.

The Common Vase

Deep in one of your cabinets in the kitchen, you have probably stockpiled an impressive collection of glass flower vases and candleholders. Usually tall, clear, and somewhat elegant, these vessels make a good variation on the rocktini theme. Simply take tumble-polished stones, preferably of the same variety, and fill the vase to the top. You can experiment and see what works best; sometimes, going with a stunning variety can work out well. Other times it is nice to use identical colors and shapes.

Common candleholders work for storing polished rocks.

The Snack Bowl

Another decorative idea is to use a low, flat glass bowl, about 10 inches across and no more than 3 inches tall, like the ones kids used for raising turtles or Grandma used to dispense candy. The contrast of smooth, polished stones with crisp, angular crystals works well, and the big, open mouth of the bowl allows for easy access to pick up and marvel at the material.

Assorted tumble-polished agates and quartz in a tray-like setting, topped with a nice ammonite fossil

Another variation on this theme is to put your common tumble-polished material in a bowl and create a small sign: LUCKY ROCKS—TAKE ONE! You will like the idea of people leaving the house with a souvenir in their pocket.

Pans and Trays

Tumble-polished material does not have to be confined to glass vessels. A wide, flat tray or ridged tabletop can also host pebbles, and the arrangement possibilities are endless.

Inlaid Stones

If you can permanently part with some of your material, consider what you can do with tumble-polished material set into grout. For example, if you were already considering remodeling the kitchen with a nice, modern granite countertop, you could create your own backsplash by pressing tumble-polished material into

Assorted tumbler material pressed into grout in order to set off large tiles

mortar and covering with matching grout. This is advanced tile work, and you might want to use the services of an experienced artisan.

Or you might consider remodeling the living room fireplace. The old white quartzite stone often used was attractive in its day but not very friendly. By inserting a wide accent band of polished agates and jaspers, the result is impressive.

Cabinets

Curio cabinets have a long and interesting history. Wikipedia has a lengthy entry about cabinets of curiosities that begins with this note:

> The term *cabinet* originally described a room rather than a piece of furniture. The first of the cabinets of curiosities were assembled in the mid-sixteenth century. The Kunstkammer of Rudolf II, Holy Roman Emperor (ruled 1576–1612), housed in the Hradschin at Prague was unrivalled north of the Alps; it provided a solace and retreat for contemplation that also served to demonstrate his imperial magnificence and power in symbolic arrangement of their display, ceremoniously presented to visiting diplomats and magnates.

Attractive cabinets with divided drawers help organize your collection.

A quick Internet search for "collection cabinet" pulled up hundreds of good links showing attractive cabinets that take your display efforts to a whole new level. For example, Great South Gems and Minerals Online Catalog offered a distinctive museum-quality cabinet with twelve racks at this link: www.greatsouth.net/miscellaneous/p-GSCC.html. The price at press time was $229, finished. You could also save by ordering the cabinet unfinished and staining it yourself to match your home's color theme.

Kaboodle.com offers the line of Bisley Collection Cabinets at www .kaboodle.com/reviews/bisley-collection-cabinets-3. These are more stylish than wood cabinets, but the price is similar.

Ikea, Scan Design, and other furniture makers all offer similar products, often for less money, so look around for the best deal. The dividers are a key accessory, as show in the photo on the previous page.

Bigger Displays

Once you have a knack for displaying your material, consider creating your own exhibit and entering it into a competition at a rock and gem show near you. The displays shown here will give you an idea of the level of quality you should aim for.

Gem show display of "rock art," with material fashioned to resemble food

Gem show display of nicely polished spheres

Labels

After a few years, it is hard to be certain where you picked up some of the stuff you collected. In addition, there is that whole issue of someone else trying to identify material when you are not around to pontificate about each piece. So work out a system of labeling your material.

For a quick field label for a bag or sample jar, use white first-aid tape and a marker with permanent ink. The classic geologist method was to put a dab of fast-drying correction fluid on a rock and then code in an ID mark. You would write down the description to match the code in a journal or diary, and you would know what the next number was by referring to the journal.

There are all kinds of labeling programs and associated tracking software for managing your collection, but for now the important thing is to get some kind of code on your obscure pieces.

Trilobase

www.trilobase.com
The Trilobase collections managing software has good features and doesn't cost much; you can even add photos.

Security

You are probably not going to be leaving around the gold nuggets and flakes that you have panned out over the years. Most serious miners keep their most valuable finds in a safety deposit box where they cannot lose them, spill them, or for some other reason find them gone. You might miss having them around in plain sight, but you have to face reality. There is no sense tempting your houseguests with valuable material.

One suggestion is to invest in a solid wall safe. You can figure out for yourself what extra insurance or security you might need; consult with your insurance agent for good advice.

End Result

Once you get started organizing your collection, you will probably become a better collector. You might even stop bringing home big yard rocks that your conscience was telling you to "leave 'er right there."

If you worry about your collection taking over your house, you have a right to be concerned. The Rice Northwest Museum in Hillsboro, Oregon, was built as a residence around a collection. Check out the web page at www.ricenwmuseum.org. This is what happens when the collection takes over—nobody actually lives here anymore!

GLOSSARY

In addition to Wikipedia and other sources:

Confidently billed as the "best ever" rockhounding resource, **Gator Girl's website** also has a solid glossary of rockhounding terms at www.gatorgirlrocks .com/resources/glossary.html.

The College of Natural Resources at the Berkeley campus of the University of California has a deep, technical reference about rocks and minerals: http://nature.berkeley.edu/classes/eps2//wisc/glossary2.html.

GoldOz has a very nice glossary of terms specific to geology and mining: www.goldoz.com.au/34.0.html.

All About Gemstones has a good glossary for rocks, crystals, and gems at www.allaboutgemstones.com/glossary_gemology.html.

Alluvium: Stream and river deposits of sand, mud, rock, and other material. Geologists and soil scientists avoid the term *dirt,* as it has no descriptive value. Alluvium is sometimes sorted if laid down in deep water; otherwise it can be unsorted if deposited during floods, earthquakes, etc. If glaciers were involved, the term *till* is used.

Anthracite: The hardest and most intensely metamorphosed form of coal. It is heavier and shinier than other types of coal and less likely to make a mess in your hands.

Arkose: Sandstone that contains mostly unsorted, broken-up pieces of feldspar and quartz; usually hard and not easily eroded.

Basement: The "lowest" and oldest rocks around—usually metamorphic and frequently dating to the Precambrian or Paleozoic in age. Although considered the basement rocks, they are usually less prone to erosion and can actually make up mountain ranges and stunning cliffs. "Basement" refers to their placement at the bottom of a stratigraphic table.

Batholith: General term that refers to extremely large masses of coarse intrusive rock, such as granite, quartz monzonite, granodiorite, or diorite, that extend over a large surface area. Anything over 100 km2 is considered a batholith. For perspective, the Idaho Batholith covers about 15,000 square miles. Other significant batholiths include the Sierra Nevada range, Pikes Peak in Colorado, Stone Mountain in Georgia, and South Mountain in Nova Scotia.

Bedding: The tendency of sedimentary rocks such as sandstone to reside in visible zones. Some bedding is marked by lighter or darker material, while other bedding zones may be sorted by grain size, from sand grains to giant boulders. The amount of time represented by individual zones can range greatly; some active lakes can lay down two beds per year, but in other cases there can be years between events that lay down a new bed.

Bleb: A round or oval cavity, air bubble, hole, or vesicle, usually in basalt; sometimes filled with opal, agate, or chalcedony.

Chemical sediment: Refers to the way certain limestones and dolomites are created when water becomes too saturated with a chemical and starts to precipitate material such as calcium carbonate, which falls to the bottom of the sea or bay and accumulates.

Clasts: Catchall term for the clay, silt, sand, gravel, cobbles, and boulders that make up nonchemical sedimentary rocks and other breccias. The size of the clasts then determines the name of the rock.

Clay: Usually refers to the smallest mineral fragments, smaller than 2μm or 1/255 millimeter. Geologists, soil scientists, sedimentologists, and geotechnical engineers can have different definitions of the split between clay and silt, however.

Cobble: Fancy term for rocks between a pebble and a boulder. The exact definition of a cobble is anything from 64 to 256 millimeters in size.

Contact metamorphism: The result of a hot igneous intrusion on the country rock it is intruding is usually to provide heat and pressure, which can cause minerals to form and change the texture of the existing rock. The contact zones between the intrusion and the surrounding rock can sometimes house interesting quartz veins and spark economic ore extraction.

Density: Since it isn't enough to measure the outright weight of two different samples, we need to define the weight per an agreed unit of density. By weighing the sample and then dunking it in water and measuring the volume of water displaced, we get the density measured in grams per cubic centimeter. The general term *heft* refers to a field test for how dense a hand specimen feels.

Diatomite: Usually a white, chalky deposit that, upon microscopic inspection, turns out to be composed of tiny diatom fossils. These beds can often host common opal, precious opal, and zeolite deposits.

Drift: General term for glacial deposits composed of jumbled debris. Outwash plains and terraces are usually sorted, whereas till, erratic, and moraines are unsorted.

Dry wash: The sign of a seasonal stream that dries up during the summer months. These can be interesting for rockhounds, as specimen sizes are usually bigger because they haven't been severely eroded.

Eolian: General term for wind deposits such as loess, sand sheets, ripples, and dunes, but it also can refer to wind processes such as dust storms, sandblasting, and desert varnish.

Eon: The longest division of geologic time is the super-eon. The model is:

super-eon → eon → era → period → epoch → age.

We are in the Holocene epoch of the Quaternary period of the Cenozoic age of the Phanerozoic eon of the Cambrian super-eon.

Epoch: Shorter subdivision of a geologic period, usually corresponding to observed stratigraphy in the field.

Era: The four main geologic eras, from oldest to youngest, are the Precambrian, Paleozoic, Mesozoic, and Cenozoic.

Erosion: The forces and processes that continually grind down mountains and move their debris downwind or downhill.

Evaporite: As bodies of water dry up under desert conditions, they frequently get white or light-brown rings around the edges. These minerals are usually salt (halite, or sodium chloride) or a related halide, but conditions can form deposits of borax or gypsum as well.

Exfoliation: This term refers to the way rocks, in particular granite, tend to slough off skins or layers of outer rock like on onion. The result is usually a rough, rounded shape rather than angles and edges.

Facies: Term introduced by Swiss geologist Amanz Gressly (1814–65) to describe how sedimentary rocks can be identified by the way they were deposited but still be the same overall rock. The term *biofacies* describes the distinct fossil assemblage, while the term *lithofacies* could describe the differences in clast size. There could be several distinct facies identifiable in the field that make up the overall formation.

Felsic: A loose term that describes light-colored, igneous rocks that are low in iron and magnesium and rich in feldspars (and quartz). The term felsite is a catchall field term, used when the exact identification of an apparently silicic rock is uncertain, rather than a name for a particular type of rock.

Float: Describes the difference between rock samples hammered from an outcrop, and thus with a known origin, and samples that exist as cobbles or boulders and not attached to bedrock. Prospectors are able to trace float to its source outcrop.

Flood basalt: Refers to the way basalt tends to pour out of cracks and vents and form rivers of liquid rock and thus create plateaus of flat, layered deposits.

Flow cleavage: Describes the tendency of metamorphic rocks to arrange flat, elongated crystals into a parallel structure.

Formation: This is a key term to understand in field geology. Geologists assign formation names to mappable, recognizable rock assemblages and also note a "type" locale that defines the rest of the unit. Formations can be lumped together into groups or even supergroups, such as the Belt Supergroup of northern Idaho, Montana, Wyoming, Washington, and British Columbia. To become a formation, a group of similar rocks must be big enough to be worth the bother, must share some key similarity, and must be traceable across the surface. Some formations are divided into members.

Geologic cycle: The continuous cycle of destruction, recycling, and rebirth that defines the way the Earth's crust works. There are countless variations on the scenario, but in general, rocks are created, such as by a volcano, eroded, built back into sedimentary deposits, subducted, turned back into lava, and erupted again.

Graded bedding: When streams cross a valley floor, they tend to drop the biggest pebbles and boulders at the bottom; as the sediments build up and the current wanes, the next bed will have smaller material. In time a complete sequence of beds gets built, graded out perfectly, with the coarsest conglomerates at the bottom and fine siltstones at the top. This bedding cycle can get repeated and makes for interesting outcrops when revealed.

Gravel: The best place for pebble pups and rockhounds to search for interesting material. Gravels usually consist of pebbles, cobbles, and boulders, in various ratios, and also contain varying amounts of sand and silt.

Hydrothermal vein: Best spot to investigate for interesting minerals. These hot, chemical-rich solutions, usually quartz, can either find an existing crack in country rock or create their own. If they cool slowly enough, hydrothermal veins can create large crystals prized by collectors.

Ignimbrite: The igneous rock created when hot volcanic ash and breccias pour out of a volcano or vent and are too heavy to drift away as an ash cloud. Instead the hot, heavy cloud pours down the slope of the mountain at great speed. If enough residual heat remains after settling, the ash bed can turn to stone and is called a lapilli tuff. Other ignimbrites remain loose and don't form into rocks.

Intrusion: Catchall term for the various granites, diorites, and related rocks that bulldoze their way through the Earth's crust but never reach the surface. Cooling in place quickly results in fine-grained material; cooling slowly gives the individual elements more time to build up into larger crystals. Understanding intrusions is a key to understanding geology, but nobody has ever witnessed an intrusion, so all our assumptions are based on field evidence and educated guesswork.

Laccolith: This is a small intrusion that squeezes in horizontally between beds and builds itself out laterally. These deposits usually have a neck, where material fed in, and a dome, depending on how forceful the intrusion was.

Lahar: When volcanic eruptions mix with melted glaciers, lakes, and snow, the result is a dangerous mudflow. The material can flow quickly, but it will soon solidify into a concrete-hard mass of jumbled ash, fragments, and pumice.

Lava: Catchall term for the molten rock that has reached the surface and includes basalt, andesite, rhyolite, dacite, etc.

Lava tube: Hollow cave or tunnel formed when flowing lava cools enough to form a crust, or ceiling, but the hot, molten material inside continues to drain downhill.

Lode: The prized zone of rich, extended mineralization that usually ensures a successful mining operation. The term is reserved for larger vein networks that cover significant ground, such as the Mother Lode gold mining district of California's Sierra Nevada.

Luster: Term for the visual appearance of a mineral's lighted surface. The way minerals reflect light can be helpful for identification, but terms such as *metallic* and *waxy* are not completely standardized.

Mafic mineral: These are the dark, heavy minerals that are rich in iron and magnesium, such as pyroxenes, amphiboles, and olivines.

Magma: The molten lava that eventually forms igneous rock when it cools. Magma that cools without eruption is called an intrusion; magma that breaks through the surface is called lava.

Magma chamber: The source cavity or reservoir for magma traveling up through the Earth's crust.

Mass spectrometer: The one instrument you wish you had, because it can count ions and provide their exact distribution. There are various technologies, but the bottom line is that a handheld mass spectrometer would revolutionize field geology.

Mohs scale of hardness: The observation-based method of ranking a mineral by what it can scratch and what, in turn, can scratch it. Diamond is alone at the top of the list at 10, and it can scratch corundum, which can scratch topaz, which can scratch quartz, at 7. The remaining minerals used as measurements on the Mohs scale are orthoclase feldspar (6), apatite (5), fluorite (4), calcite (3), gypsum (2), and talc, the softest (1).

Native metal: Metals in their purest form are not significantly combined with oxides, sulfides, carbonates, or silicates and are thus native. Gold, silver, copper, platinum, and mercury are examples of metals sometimes found in their native condition.

Oil shale: A dark, organic-rich shale that sometimes contains enough petroleum-based ingredients to burn. Massive oil shale deposits in Canada and Wyoming probably hold astonishing amounts of oil, but extraction will be expensive and environmentally risky.

Oolite: Refers to the small, round form taken when calcium carbonates start to coat sand grains and roll around in a lime-rich sea bottom and continually build up from small pellets to marble size or larger. These little round grains sometimes form an easily identified oolitic limestone.

Ore: The term used to describe a viable mineral deposit that is worth mining. Usually refers to a metals-based mineral that must be milled.

Original Horizontality: This term refers to the idea proposed by Nicholas Steno (1638–86) that sedimentary rocks are laid down flat. Since many sandstone beds are currently tilted, this simple concept meant other forces were at work and paved the way for theories on mountain building that eventually led to plate tectonics and more.

Outcrop: A cliff, ledge, or other visible clue to the rock formations below.

Pegmatite: A key igneous rock, usually found as a vein or dike, with very large grains of mica, feldspar, and tourmaline, among others. Pegmatites tends to form cavities and vugs where large crystals can accumulate without crowding into one another and damaging their crystal structure. Pegmatites sometimes host smoky quartz, beryl, topaz, aquamarine, and other gems.

Pelagic sediment: Catchall term for the fine sediments that slowly accumulate in deep marine environments. Rather than relying on silt or clastic debris, this material is predominantly derived from shells of microscopic organizations such as foraminifera. Accumulation rates are as slow as 0.1 centimeter per 1,000 years.

Reaction series: Refers to the behavior of a cooling magma where some minerals form at high temperature. But as the magma cools further, that early mineral may dissolve and reform as a new, different mineral. These conditions are observable in a laboratory setting.

Regolith: Another catchall term, this time describing the various rock fragments and erosional debris that lie on bedrock, including alluvium, clastics, etc.

Replacement deposit: Describes a particular type of ore deposit where hot, circulating solutions first dissolve a mineral to form a cavity and then fill the void with a new material.

Sedimentary structure: Groups the various relicts of a sedimentary rock's deposition, such as ripples, cracks, and bedding.

Stratification: The tendency of sedimentary rocks to form in flat, parallel sequences that are mappable at the surface for considerable distances. After long study, geologists can easily identify patterns and start to unravel the sequence of events represented in the strata.

Stratigraphic column: Stratigraphy is the science and study of sedimentary rock outcrops. Stratigraphers create elegant stratigraphic columns that pictorially represent the measured or inferred relations of rock outcrops, measuring the thickness of groups, formations, and members. Metamorphic and igneous rocks occasionally show up in stratigraphic columns, but stratigraphy is primarily a tool to understand sedimentary rocks.

Streak: Refers to the color of the powdered mineral dust left behind when a mineral is scraped across a streak plate. The color of this fine rock powder is a truer reflection of the mineral than visual appearance. Since a streak plate is about 7 on the Mohs hardness scale, only minerals less than a hardness of 7 can be tested by streak.

Superposition, Principle of: Another theory traced to Nicolas Steno, who pointed out that except for rare instances where geologic forces have tilted, folded, and severely disrupted the bedrock, a formation or stratum that sits on top of another distinct layer must be younger than the rock below. Except in rare conditions, the older rock will be at the bottom.

Talus: The impressive accumulation of debris below a cliff or prominent outcrop. Because the rocks are shifting constantly and continuing to accumulate, few plants can get a foothold. Also called scree.

Tectonics: Geologic theories of how the Earth's crust continually moves and shapes new rocks. To compare planets, on Mars there is little evidence of tectonics, and there is basically one volcano, Olympus Mons, rising 21 kilometers above the planet's surface. Presumably, a single hot spot continually fed this one massive volcano. On Earth the plates continually shift; as one example, in Hawaii we see dozens of volcanic islands that have erupted as the plates pass above a single, long-lived hot spot.

Texture: Describes a rock's grain size, crystal size, if the grains are uniform or variable, if the grains are rounded or angular, and if there is any evidence of orientation to the grains.

Till: Jumbled mess of glacial debris, with little to no recognizable bedding present and sediment sizes ranging from rock flour and clay all the way to massive boulders.

Tuff: The term used to describe ash, pumice, volcanic breccias, and other debris. These ash beds can often be an excellent source for petrified wood and fossil leaves. Given enough residual heat after settling down, tuffs can cook themselves into a "welded tuff" that is extremely hard and resistant to erosion and usually lacks identifiable fossils.

Ultramafic rock: Igneous rocks such as dunite, peridotite, amphibolite, and pyroxenite that consist of primarily mafic minerals and have less than 10 percent feldspar.

Vein: An intruded mineral-rich solution that froze into place by following a crack, fault, or other zone of weakness. Veins are usually made up of quartz, but can be calcite, feldspar, or other minerals. Veins often carry in sulfides, precious metals, and other compounds of interest to miners and gem collectors.

Volcanic ash: The fine rock fragments and glassy, angular material ejected from a volcano into the air. Instead of forming flows, magma can sometimes be met with violent escaping gasses, resulting in clouds of ash that can travel significant distances or even circle the Earth.

Volcanic breccia: A pyroclastic rock made up of angular fragments that show little or no sign of waterborne movement. Particle sizes are greater than 2 millimeters in diameter.

Vug: A pocket or hollow seam where crystals have an opportunity to increase their size without interfering greatly with the growth of the crystals next to them. Vugs in pegmatites often contain beryl, emeralds, and other precious gems.

Xenolith: Literally, "foreign rock," where a piece of country rock is picked off the walls or otherwise incorporated into a rising or spreading dike or intrusion.

Zeolite: Common aluminosilicates formed in volcanic rocks, such as basalt, where alkaline groundwater circulates at low temperature and creates a ringed "molecular sieve" structure. Very useful for filtering contaminants and absorbing odors.

INDEX